a million pieces
in a
thousand places

a million pieces in a thousand places

GERARD MCLEAN

Sharktooth Press

Copyright © 2024 by Gerard McLean

All rights reserved worldwide.

No part of this book may be reproduced in any form or by any electronic or mechanical means, including information storage and retrieval systems, without written permission from the author, except for the use of brief quotations in a book review.

All attempts at finding typos have been employed, but if one or two escaped capture, treat it kindly.

Printed in the United States of America

Library of Congress Control Number: 2024944339

PRINT: 978-1-7353989-5-2
EPUB: 978-1-7353989-6-9

Sharktooth Press
Kingston, New York USA

www.sharktoothpress.com

10 9 8 7 6 5 4 3 2

No idea what I'm doing but I had pie for breakfast this morning and called it pastry. It's a start.

CONTENTS

1. BBQ at the Hendersons — 1
2. Connections in the stars — 3
3. How to hide a body — 5
4. The life of bread — 7
5. Nothing to do, nowhere to go — 9
6. From caterpillar to book — 11
7. Object impermanence — 13
8. Permanent impermanence — 15
9. Blown to bits, scattered to the million corners of the internets — 19
10. My writing mask — 21
11. In the present — 23
12. Member, partner — 25
13. Rain — 27
14. Terms of engagement — 29
15. At least nobody died tonight — 31
16. Patience — 35
17. What if God* does make mistakes — 39
18. On change — 45
19. A small life — 47
20. A dead squirrel — 51
21. 59 1/2 years — 53
22. Rusting away — 55
23. The value of old men — 57
24. The Patriarch — 59
25. Your dog doesn't know you are mentally unstable — 63
26. My neighborhood died — 67
27. It's about time — 69
28. The flower and the dirt — 71
29. My letter to Marc Lacey at the New York Times — 73
30. What do you NOT write about? — 77
31. The poetry of journalism — 79

32.	The Corn and the Carrot	81
33.	Skowhegan	83
34.	Dead by fifty	85
35.	Candle flame	87
36.	My neutral face	89
37.	Hope, fire and dirt	91
38.	Husky	93
39.	Beginnings	95
40.	Bike grease	97
41.	Impatient	99
42.	Selling	103
43.	Inkstained	105
44.	Soccer kicks in	109
45.	The rules of a job	113
46.	Inanimate me	115
47.	Hitting the ground running	119
48.	What is the wheelbase of a cat?	125
49.	The smell of sun and warm bodies	127
50.	The real sh*t	131
	About Gerard	139
	Also by Gerard Mclean	141

1

BBQ AT THE HENDERSONS

Mr. and Mrs. Henderson are my backyard neighbors who have lived in the house across the fence a few years before I moved in. I've been here for thirty-one years. Their kids have long flown, so it's just him, her and their dog, Sally, who is a bit blind and barks at shadows. Mr. Henderson loves to grill and built himself a backyard fire pit. He burns a fire almost every night.

The Hendersons mostly keep to themselves, but occasionally they'll have friends over, especially when Mr. Henderson gets a new load of logs delivered. He likes to split and stack his own wood.

"A man needs to know how to tend his own fire, how to stack wood so it dries out properly," he has said more than once. "Otherwise, your fire gets too smoky if the wood is green."

Mr. Henderson is getting older and he sometimes forgets things, but he knows his wood.

It was on the occasion of a wood delivery that Mr. and Mrs. Henderson invited me and a few neighbors to a BBQ. As we gathered, Mr. Henderson stoked the fire to a roaring blaze. I had never seen him build a fire this large before, but the air was chilly and we were grateful as the sun had set an hour or so ago.

"Where is Mrs. Henderson?" we asked. "Inside seasoning the steaks," he replied. "She'll be with us shortly," and he promptly refreshed our beers.

The chatter turned to matters of fall cleanup, when was the last day the town will pick up leaves, how to prepare rose bushes for the winter, what the kids are doing these days, why they visit less and less... as Mr. Henderson busied himself with more logs and refreshing our beers.

We were getting hungry.

"I should go see what's keeping Mrs. Henderson with the meat." He trudged into the house to check on his wife.

A few minutes later, he emerged on the back deck, carrying a platter of seasoned steaks. We each stabbed into one and slapped it on the searing hot grill. A few minutes later, famished, we each tore into the steak.

"Delicious." "Perfectly seasoned." "Medium rare is the only way to go."

It was then I noticed Mrs Henderson hadn't yet joined us. "What's keeping your wife," I asked. "She's missing a great BBQ."

"Oh, she's here with us," Mr Henderson said as he cut a slice of meat off his steak, put it in his mouth, leaning back with a sigh as he chewed.

This is a work of fiction.

2

CONNECTIONS IN THE STARS

On September 2, 2004, a man almost nobody heard of[1] outside his peer group, climbed a media scaffold in Springfield, Ohio and started filming the political speech John Kerry was delivering to the crowd. Within minutes, he was having a heart attack. The paramedics reached him, but not in time to save his life.

He was more than a newspaper man. He was a philosopher, a thinker, a dreamer and a very good friend. He opened his heart, mind and soul to this cocky, inquisitive artist from the second floor who kept bothering him at the end of the day... or showing up at lunchtime with no purpose other than to talk about everything and nothing.

He always had time.

A friend sent me this quote out of the blue the other day. It reminded me of Jeff.

> "Although I am a typical loner in daily life, my consciousness of belonging to the invisible community of those who strive for truth, beauty, and justice keeps me from feeling isolated." — Albert Einstein

When I was working at the *Dayton Daily News*, we produced a Newspaper in Eduction page on constellations. His wife—who is the director of astronomy at our local planetarium—was a consultant

---

1. Jeff Adams, Photo Director at the *Dayton Daily News*

for me on that page. Her enthusiasm for the stars was infectious and wove itself into the fabric of my indelible memories.

Jeff died young, but he is with me almost every night when I venture out to walk my dogs. When the sky is clear, I look up to count the stars in Orion's Belt, then drift north to locate the Pleiades.

When the sky is cloudy over Dayton, Ohio and I cannot see Orion, I get anxious about losing a connection to a soul who understood mine without words. I feel the ground shift under me and my heart races to find a handrail to anchor the irrational terror I will die having established no purpose, no connection to humanity.

Silly, I know, yet....

3

HOW TO HIDE A BODY

MURDERING SOMEONE; that's the easy part. Just point the gun and shoot. The harder part of the whole endeavor, as every seasoned assassin knows, is hiding the body.

I speak in metaphor, of course. Please, don't go shooting someone. It's not really a nice thing to do and most folks get annoyed when they're shot at.

I'm talking about books. I buy too many books and have a hard time hiding the bodies. At first, I just placed them on the bookshelf like they have always been there. But like any landfill or dumpster you throw a body into, the shelves started filling up.

A lot of books now come from Amazon, shipped in coffins of various construction. Sometimes when I get a lot of pulp corpses shipped all at once, the coffin is massive and I need to break it down and bury the book coffin in separate graveyards, apart from the books.

I need to strategically stagger my crimes.

I also find myself delaying the bibliocide until the middle of the week, to insure the body doesn't show up in the USPS Sunday delivery. It's hard to hide a body while family and friends are home eating after-church lunch.

I guess I could reform and buy digital bits. Bits are like ashes, easier to store in plain sight without friends and family suspecting you are hiding bodies.

I need an alibi.

Clap so the authorities know we were dancing with

each other at Club Substack when the crime went down. They will probably start with my follow list.

We should get our stories straight now.

4

THE LIFE OF BREAD

> Warm slice
> Sandwich
> Toast
> Croutons
> Crumbs
> Duck food
> Penicillin

5

NOTHING TO DO, NOWHERE TO GO

THE HIBISCUS OPENED UP OVERNIGHT. Sitting on the deck with my dog, Zoey, birds singing, breezes, coffee, music and flowers.

It might rain.

Thinking about the time right before we all had cell phones and cameras at the ready, how we couldn't take a photo of flowers or dogs or look up the weather or pull up a tune and we sat with ourselves and felt the things. We made memories we would not accurately recall years later, everything out of time and place even as the feeling was undeniably accurate. The music came through a radio, cassette, vinyl if we were lucky to have these things but mostly songs played in your head from memories made earlier.

We passed the time by reading and singing and talking and smoking and sex, because there was always another hour, another day and nothing was urgent that didn't come through the ring on a telephone wired in the next room that you maybe didn't hear or you ignored.

None of this made money and none of it felt unproductive or frivolous.

We made music by playing chords over and over and over on our guitars and harmonicas because there was no notification of a new email pinging at us. We were in a measure or a hook for hours upon hours to get it right, undistracted by the call of TikTok or Instagram. We were contently anxious ... or anxiously content ... in our boredom, our time focused on becoming good at listening, thinking, playing music, reading

Now we're all chasing one distraction after another. Instead of sitting with the hibiscus flowers, we take a photo, write some dumb nostalgic caption and post that shit on Instagram, our minds already onto the other thing we're probably not gonna get done today.

6

FROM CATERPILLAR TO BOOK

ON SEPTEMBER 5TH, a caterpillar started spinning a chrysalis on my front porch to begin her journey into becoming a butterfly. It wasn't the ideal place for her to do this, but she didn't know that. She couldn't see the bigger picture, but I could.

So for the next ten days or so, nature put me in charge of making sure she was going to emerge a butterfly at the other end. I waited and watched.

On September 15th, she emerged from her chrysalis a gorgeous orange and black monarch butterfly. As life goes, she had flown off while I ducked inside for a few minutes and it felt sad that I didn't get a chance to say a proper goodbye.

But the next day, as I was taking my dog Zoey out for a walk, she flew back into my garden! It's as if she was coming back to thank me for taking care of her during her most vulnerable state of her life.

I know this is just a butterfly, but for this one little butterfly, her entire life depended on me sharing a small part of my world and keeping her safe.

FROM A CASUAL OBSERVATION above one summer day that lasted ten, a butterfly named Callie found her way into a children's book.

The story that follows is how a caterpillar watch turned into a book.

Last year, I noticed a caterpillar had made herself into a chrysalis on my front porch railing. I published my story and made a short video which caught Sarah Woodard's eye. She commented that it would make a great story for one of her books.

I agreed.

But here is the really, super cool part for me; she actually WROTE the book! I gotta say, Carlos Lopez, the illustrator, made me out to be way more handsome that I am and Sarah wrote me to be more heroic than I was. Not gonna lie, that second to the last page made me tear up a bit.

Of course I bought three right away—one for me which I'm not lending out—and one for each of my grandkids' libraries. You should go and buy one today... or as many copies as you have kids or grandkids! The title is *Callie's Change*.

If there is any lesson here, it is these two things, at least for me:

- Keep putting stuff out into the world. You never know where the magic will land.
- If you are lucky enough to receive magic, embrace it, listen to it and do something with it. The magic you transform will become something exponentially beautiful and inspire others to continue the magic.

7

OBJECT IMPERMANENCE

When I was about 9 or 10 or maybe 8, I can't recall, it has been a long time.... I was obsessed with chess, like *The Queens Gambit* obsessed... I borrowed a book about chess from the local library on Lexington and University in St Paul. It's not there any more, I don't know... it's probably a restaurant or something...

That's not really the point, other than if I'm not there directing change, change never happens for the better. That's how important I am.

The point is I let the due date slip by, then I hid the book because I wanted to believe I had lost it instead of really wanting to keep it and read it over and over and over to get really good at chess. Really good at something. Then it got too late to actually return it and I had forgotten where I hid it. Life moved on, the St Paul Public Library gave up trying to extract the book or the replacement money from me. Maybe they closed and just lost track of me.

Ten or so years later, my parents lost their only house they could afford to a foreclosure and I returned to my old room to clear out what little of my childhood I wanted to keep. That room had become my younger sister's room when I ... escaped... at seventeen. I'm not sure what would have been left that was mine, but the exercise seemed to be important to my mom.

I found the book I had hid in my little private space I created in the closet between the walls. I had long forgotten about that "closet," but it was a bit of a time capsule of what I held so close to my heart when I was young, the small objects of my youth I was deathly afraid others would take from me, those things that would leave me incomplete, despondent and perhaps a bit... suicidal ... if I had to live without them.

So... I'm still here. I hope you are, too.

8

PERMANENT IMPERMANENCE

I BOUGHT an old '60s rotary telephone last week. I don't really know why, but I think I do. It is a physical object that at one point defined the concept of "home," a place where your life was a permanent thing. You lived where you could plug in a phone and people could call you at. It only rang at one place.

I know, this concept did not exist at some point in human existence, but the phone then was something else, maybe the place where you could stable your horse. But it was always a "physical" place of some sort. Even nomads had a "place" where they could rest, repair, belong.

I'm thinking lately about the concept of permanent impermanence. I'm not quite sure what to do with these thoughts or what they mean in a larger concept of capitalism and the human need for certainty. I'm not looking for answers or solutions on how to find stability in a world that changes faster than our ability to control our destiny. I'm just ruminating.

I watched the movie *Nomadland* last night and what it means for Fern and all of us who are living in a culture that has expectations of a stable home vs our need to explore. On the one hand, we're encouraged to seek out new experiences, but when we try, we're bum-rushed out of spaces that feed this need. We can't just park a van any place we are; we have to pay for the space. Even what looks like a stretch of desert in the middle of nowhere, someone owns it. Someone is going to bang on your van door and tell you to move along unless you shell out some money.

We should have a job, a house, a family around us.

I hesitate buying a new book because I will have to place it on a bookshelf in a place that feels less and less permanent. I feel the same as my finger hovers over the "Buy Now" button on Amazon or various websites when I feel like I need a new trinket or gadget. If I buy this thing, I get to hold it but I also need to put it somewhere, a somewhere that feels increasingly like a place that is not mine.

I was given a theater-sized popcorn popper a few years back as a birthday gift. It gave me a lot of joy being able to pop popcorn anytime I wanted. After a few months, the popcorn popper went from something that sparked joy to something that just stunk up the house and probably attracted mice. I reluctantly moved it from the house into the garage where it now sits. I am allowed to make a batch of popcorn when the house is empty. It's been several months since I've made popcorn as my house is hardly ever my space lately. Besides, I want to make sure my current pant size is either permanent or reduced and massive amounts of buttered popcorn work against that goal.

My dad was a philosopher when he was sober. I carry an image burned into my brain of him sitting alone at the head of the dining room table in the house I grew up. It was the middle of the day, but the room was dark because the black bomb curtains were drawn. The room was filled with smoke from the pack of cigarettes he was finishing off and the cherry of his lit cigarette glowed as he inhaled.

"Like footsteps on a sandy dune," he said, holding his arms out and slowly bringing them back in to take another drag of his cigarette. "All of this—of me—will be blown away in the wind, like footsteps on a sandy dune." He seemed profoundly sad and broken. I remember thinking that should be the title of his book. Years later when it became apparent he would never write it, I thought it should be the title of my book.

He died at 85, not written that book. I still haven't years later.

I want what Hester Pryne had at the end of The Scarlet Letter—a small home, the quiet of stability... (oops, spoiler alert for every high school student who never got past the "A" in the novel and wrote song lyrics without the proper context... sorry Taylor, I love ya, but the reference is ... confused...) But even the house you paid off is never quite yours because you have to pay the property taxes and the threat of a shifting "free market" makes a house not really yours.

Maybe the permanence is now the glowing screens of my MacBookPro and my iPhone, found at the address of gerardmclean.com and @gerardmclean at various points on the interwebs and not at the terminated end of a phone wire.

See you on down the road.

9

BLOWN TO BITS, SCATTERED TO THE MILLION CORNERS OF THE INTERNETS

A MILLION PIECES in a thousand places...

I woke up today and I had had enough; enough of the algorithms that did not guide me to find the stuff I liked, but actively scattered my existence into the million corners of the internets. Stop it, stop it right now! I am aware that saying a million corners is silly but just ... shut up! you are part of my problem...

Time and place are context. Time and place are context. Time and place are context.

Who gave you permission to take every bit of content on the planet and burst it apart into million pieces and force me to spend the better part of my morning trying to glue back everything so it make sense?

A conversation with another human being isn't a disruptive flow of crap from every sewage line everywhere just because I searched for "Roto-rooter, help me, it's 3am and OMGOD the smell!" five months ago. The problem has been fixed, the smell is... OMGod, yes, Amazon, it's a goddam metaphor, you hulking pile of stupid!

Now Medium, my quiet corner in the middle of chaos, has apparently embraced the hyper-algorithm. I found stories I liked, but when I refreshed the screen (or more accurately, it got refreshed for me) I lost the story. Hopelessly lost in the morass of crap, spewing from the latest sewage line that started in Gary Vaynerchuk's basement, probably. (Stop it, Amazon. I already bought his latest book. Butt the hell out!)

The breaking point came this morning when I couldn't even find my own stuff on Medium. I know I had written a piece and had a vague recollection of the title, but I could not for the life of me, find the damn thing. I still can't. But I made an ad hoc index and this is what will stand until Medium realizes that physical time and place is also context and content.

Place matters. Place influences how you see the world and how accessible you are to the world. People need anchors and a sense of place. Potential customers need to know you really, really exist beyond a website and email address. Nothing establishes that like place.

If you are ever in town and want to dine on omelettes from a styrofoam to-go clamshell, in a van with three dogs, parked outside a Bob Evans, look me up.

10

MY WRITING MASK

I dread offending people.

Some people use that against me to keep me in line, to keep me between the lines they drew, the kinds they feel outline the straight and narrow they want me to walk within. Rarely do I get asked if I want to walk on this path, I'm only supposed to know that I want that. That path is the way normal, well-adjusted adult men walk.

Conform to that, dammit, you are embarrassing yourself... you are embarrassing me.

I don't want most of what I am told I should at my age. A big house, a steady job, a newer car, a non-dysfunctional relationship with my siblings, grandkids...

Is everything ok with him? I saw he wrote a thing that seems a little... he didn't mention you at all... that seems odd... he should mention you.

The story isn't about you. You don't have the right to tell me what I should write. You are why I wear a mask.

But I don't write what my soul aches to say. I edit myself to fit behind my writer mask, with my face poking out just a little bit to lure you into my stories; but in a benign way. I never intend to lie to you for any other reason than to connect our mutual humanity. The me you see behind my writer mask is the real me, just not the whole me.

That is not fair! We want to see the real you, not the you hiding behind a mask. I thought I knew you but you are just another liar on the internet.

You never will see the whole real me. I will always wear a mask even as many of my readers may feel I share my soul freely. I don't; I gauge the ability of my audience to absorb what I share and push just a little bit more, attempting to induce a feeling of being overwhelmed. But that is easy for me; too easy sometimes.

Don't you feel guilt about manipulating people? You can't just toy with people like they are your little playthings. That is selfish and reckless. You are gaslighting them...

I struggle with seduction all the time. Am I sharing this to seduce you into getting what I want? Is this ethical? Is seduction ever kind? Are you doing the same with me by reading and clicking my heart? Is this a fair exchange of attention? Are we both equally lonely, circling each other, searching for cues of mutual attraction? Do I need to interact with you with one hand on my sidearm, knowing I have to shoot at you if you outdraw me? Are you seducing me?

I benefit from people around me who find me tedious, my writing uninspired, too existential and not pragmatic enough. Everything has to do something, be worth a comparative return in real worth. An essay doesn't do anything; tweets, threads, notes, instagrams don't draw a paycheck. They don't go out of their way to read me, but they might. Their world view needs my mask. Even me peeking out from the edges this much threatens their world. It threatens who they believe they are by defining who they need me to be.

Is this story a mask? You, dear reader, need to figure that out for yourself; I've told you all I'm gonna say, which has already been too much.

11

IN THE PRESENT

I FORGET what we talked about yesterday unless I write it down.

I won't go through my photos on my phone and catalog them. They happened yesterday and I captured them for that moment, in that moment.

I can't write a memoir. Recalling yesterday takes time away from today.

My MacBook Pro desktop is littered with screenshots I took to illustrate that story I wrote yesterday.

I can't edit video or audio. More accurately, I hate editing video or audio. I'd much rather keep at it until I get a clean take.

I love (old Twitter) now Threads because it loves "now." I get anxious when I download my archive that contains hundreds of thousands of tweets I popped off in the moment of my yesterdays. Others might want to recall tweets for a #TBT bit, but I can never find that moment I kinda remember. So I just keep tweeting forward, but saving the archives. Maybe others will want to reconstruct me some day. I doubt it.

When someone asks for my portfolio or a writing sample, I get anxious about the work involved pulling it together. It takes away from my present and my future.

My Medium, Substack, personal blogs are littered with stories I had forgotten I'd written, under noms de plum I had forgotten I had.

Did I say that? Did I tell you that? Was that you who shared that experience with me? Where did we do that?

Who was I? I remembered the past so much more clearly as a young man. Now, I find it safer for my sanity to just live my present. There is much less clutter in the now.

If I say I love you or I trust you, I'm sincere today, in this moment, regardless of what tomorrow brings.

This story will be forgotten by me when I hit publish. I will only be reminded I wrote it when a reader likes, highlights or comments on it.

But for now, I'm still here.

12

MEMBER, PARTNER

I DON'T REALLY WANT to be a member or a partner. I just want to hang in a safe, comfortable place from time to time with people who like and trust me, where the doors are never locked because they don't need to be. Where nobody demands the rent every month and we all take care of each other.

I don't want to worry if I'm pulling my weight or taking more than I'm allowed; that others are taking more from me than they are giving back. I want to live on the wider arc, that we are all here for each other, that what affects you, affects me. Where there is music and words and poetry and dance and art because these things are the food the soul craves. Where there is no fear or anxiety resulting from something intimate we shared with another human being.

But eventually, it always comes down to money. When life is a transaction, it gets selfish. Even at five bucks a month.

13

RAIN

If you find me in the rain without an umbrella, leave me be.

I'm feeling a memory.

14

TERMS OF ENGAGEMENT

I want to be known as being kind.
I want to be seen as smart.
I want others to know I care deeply about their pain and happiness.
I want to be proud of others' success.
I want to be trusted.
But I will not be messed with.
Do not mistake my kindness for weakness; I will beat your ass into the ground in the most brutal way possible if you do.
But I will apologize and help you stand up again afterwards, if you'll let me.
Because I want to be known as being kind.

15

AT LEAST NOBODY DIED TONIGHT

Warning, ideation and self-harm imagery is contained within. Stop here if this is unhealthy for you to read.

WHEN YOU ABRUPTLY SAY "GOOD BYE" the first thing that happens is people panic... what does this mean? are you leaving for the day? When will you be back? WILL you be back? Are you going to kill yourself? OMG YOU ARE!

"Who do we call? I only have your DM." off to your website, scour it for a phone number as I shake, call the local police that I know the city you live in. And there is a knock on the door, you know what that is.. you know your people; they panic, and they leave you wondering who this wellness check is on the other side of your door... are they checking up on you or are they reassuring themselves that their own lives are ok if you are ok? Who is this wellness check for? You greet the young man through the door, his badge catches a glint of light from your porch lamp, in your periphery, I see another officer with him... but you don't as much see her as feel her. Why is she with him? What do they want? What do they REALLY want? Certainly not to be standing on the doorstep of an old man, checking up on yet another middle-aged white man who is staring into the empty future where he has no purpose, no real love beyond what he can produce, conditional, transactional ...everything has a price to be negotiated where he will lose, he knows he'll lose, it's just a question of "by how much?" Still, this young man with a badge and & gun...

did I mention the gun? Yeah, always a gun. The first thing you realize on a "wellness check" is people who feel hopeless don't care about dying you, them, both, they just don't care and so you know you just need to walk out of this alive. Maybe that is what the second officer was there for, to make sure this young man with a badge, went home alive tonight.

What does this young men who is inviting you outside for a chat know about life? What could he possibly tell you that your lived reality doesn't already scream in your head at 3am, The Devil's Hour ...I don't know why I said this aside, we both know what goes on at 3am and who owns that time... "Do I have to speak to you?" "No, I'm just checking to see you are ok... people are worried about you..." "Are they? or are they worried about themselves?" and you shut the door. He is relentless and calls your cell phone. please leave me alone. hang up and he calls again... please, please, leave me alone. Maybe he forgot about you at the next traffic stop, maybe you were on his mind all night and into the day... maybe he quietly drives by your house every night and says a quiet prayer for you. Maybe a lot of things that are possible for his future but not yours. You and he both know where this will end, for you both... he was looking into his future as you were staring into your past

Men know these things and to expect them to tell each other while standing on a dimly lit porch on a random Thursday night, would break them both.

Today, they were merely wounded and they will survive—scarred a bit—but they each know they are on a path of a lot of yesterdays when they were standing on a dimly lit porch desperate to share their thoughts end fears, hoping the other might ease the weight but not daring to step beyond the badge, the gun, knowing better at least nobody died tonight

AT LEAST NOBODY DIED TONIGHT | 33

```
When you abruptly say "good bye" the first thing that happens is people
panic... what does this mean? are you leaving for the day? when will you
be back? WILL you be back? Are you going to kill yourself? OMG YOU ARE!
Who do we call? I only have your IM... off to your encoure, scour it for
a phone number as I shake, call the local police that I know the city
you live in. And there is a knock on the door, you know what that is...
you know your people; the panic, and they leave you wondering who this
wellness check is on the other side of your door... are they checking up
on you or are they reassuring themselves that their own lives are ok
if you are ok? who is this wellness check for? You greet the young men
through the door, his badge catches a glint of light from your porch
lamp, in your periphery, I see another officer with him... but you don't
as much see her as feel her. Why issue with him? what do they want? what
do they REALLY want? Certainly not ////// to be standing on the doorstep
of an old man, checking up on yet another middle-aged white man who is
staring into the empty future where he has no purpose, no real love beyond
what he can produce, conditional, transactional...everything has a price
to be negotiated where he will lose, he knows he'll lose, it's just a
question of "by how much?" Still, this young men with a badge and a gun...
did I mention the gun? Yeah, always a gun. The first thing you realize
on a "wellness check" is people who feel hopeless don't care about dying
you, them, both, they just don't ///// care and so you know you just need
to walk out of this alive, maybe that is what the second officer was there
for, to make sure this young man with a badge, went home alive tonight.
What does /// this young man who is inviting you//// outside for a chat
know about life? What could he possibly tell you that you lived reality
doesn't already scream in you're head at 2am, The Devil's Hour ... I don't
know why I said this aside, we both know what goes on at 2am and who owns
that time... "Do I have to speak to you?" "No, I'm just checking to see
you are ok. people are worried about you......" "Are they, or are they jo/
worried ////// about themselves and you shut the door, he is relentless
and calls your cell phone, please leave me alone, hang up and he calls
again... please, please, leave me alone. Maybe he forgot about you at the
next traffic stop, maybe //////// you were on his mind all night and into
the day... maybe he quietly drives by your house every night and says a
quiet prayer for you. Maybe a lot of things that are possible for his
future but not yours. You and he both know where this will end, for you
both... he was looking into his future as you were staring into your past
men know these things and to expect them to tell each other while standing
on a dimly lit porch on a random thursday night would break them both.
Today, they were merely wounded and they will survive -- scarred a bit --
but they each know they are on a path of a lot of yesterdays when they
were standing on a dimly lit porch desperate to share their thoughts and
fears, hoping the other might /// ///// ease the weight but not daring
to step beyond the badge, the gun, knowing better at least nobody died tonight
```

Essay part of the typewriter in a square project by the author.

16

PATIENCE

"Wait your turn," they say at every turn.

"Your house may be expensive now, but when you find yourself in mid-life, it will be less so," they say when they sell you the house. "You'll be earning more, you'll have paid down the mortgage and it will be yours." Only they never tell you your taxes and insurance will eclipse your principal payments by twice. You wouldn't have heard it anyway through the excitement of a new home, some place you can shape into your own.

They never tell you the expenses to repair the sidewalk and replace the main sewer line will be over ten percent of your house value. They never tell you the debt you go into for the repairs will never really be paid off before some other major repair is due. They never say the county will take your entire house if you miss a property tax payment that is equal to a couple mortgage payments. They never tell you they will divide up your mortgage into derivatives without your permission—except for the fine print on page 462—and sell them as junk bonds on the stock market, crashing the economy, absconding with the cash and dragging the value of your house with it.

"Patience," they say.

"Give us time to improve the ACA to include you in the Middle," they say. "Be there for us today to take care of the young and the poor…and trust that we will take care of you later." Only tomorrow never comes… a new president is whisked into office and the promises evaporate like a fart in the wind. The premiums skyrocket to twice your housing costs and three times your mortgage. Your health insurance premium is now your largest single monthly expense and it doesn't even buy an hour of actual health care.

You feel trapped in a system, in a State that no longer values you as economically viable, yet you can't really leave because outside of the State, nobody wants you either. You're too old and besides, the sale of your house isn't even enough to make a down payment in an area with any real jobs.

Medicare and Social Security, pay into it now and trust we will take care of you when you are older and can no longer work for income.

"Patience," they say.

Lies. All lies to keep you working to feed the beast, to fund the big pile of cash they will legislate away from you as if you did not earn it, working the past half-century. But you discover the lies too late. You are old and crippled, defenseless against the beast.

Deductibles that you paid, a customer of your health insurance company for fifteen years, are worthless. You discover you have no value except the month-to-month premium you pump out.

You pause in the wine aisle at Kroger, thinking maybe it would be easier to live out your remaining years as a drunk. Not today, you think, perhaps tomorrow.

Representative Democracy, they will claim. You gave us permission to make these decisions for you. Only you didn't because you are one small blue dot in a sea of red. They do not see you as a person, only as a blip in the crowd. Most of the time, they don't even see you as human, just an annoying animal that is irrationally enraged.

"Patience," they say.

It's already Thursday in a month that is more than half over. You've worked every day, but produced little to nothing. You are treading water in an economy that values volume over substance.

All you want is a place to live without anxiety, a chance to not die from some treatable cause, to live with dignity, to be respected for the contributions you've made, to share in the rewards that you believed would be there if you just paid it forward.

All they see is an old man who wants free stuff.

"Patience," they say.

"How long do we have to wait," you say. "We've lived most of our lives already."

17

WHAT IF GOD* DOES MAKE MISTAKES

I'VE SURVIVED the coronavirus pandemic. You're reading this now, so chances are, you have also survived the pandemic. Whether that turns out to be a good thing or a bad thing for each of us remains to be seen. To date, over 950,000 Americans and 6 million people world-wide have not survived.

They died. They are dead.

What if I was not supposed to survive? There is a certain comfort in dying in a mass shooting, a war, natural disaster or a pandemic. The numbers are so staggering that the individual dead get lost in the crowd.

Nobody left alive really shares the individual grief of those left behind. The grief is so overwhelming that it's easy to assume there is no grief suffered by the living. It's hard for the survivors to demand sympathy for fear of being selfish, so in some respects, everyone heals faster.

Some don't even feel, the grief is so overwhelming.

I think about the movie *The Butterfly Effect* a lot and not in a good way. Well, maybe in a matter-of-fact sort of way. The director's cut that ends with Evan traveling back to that moment his mother is about to give birth to him and he strangles himself in the womb with his umbilical cord.

He realizes that all his friends would be better off if there never was any version of him alive.

I often wonder if the same is true of me.

Now, there are clearly problems with the premise. If I did not exist, then my kids would not exist and the grandkids... but I'm not absolutely certain that is true. Perhaps they still would have existed because perhaps God* wanted them to be born. I would just not have been their dad or grandpa, but their essence—their souls, if you will—would have become part of this world. It's like wrapping your head around infinity; you can try but it will drive you insane.

I'm not an easy person to have a relationship with. I know this about myself. I'm opinionated, strong-willed and like things the way I like things, especially when it involves a creative endeavor. I have a short fuse and a bit of a temper when you push my boundaries after I have been clear about what they are. I'm slow to trust anyone and even when I do trust, it's not a deep trust. I live in a state of constant situational awareness.

As exhausting as I am to those around me, it's exponentially exhausting to be me. "Surely," I think to myself, "this is not a normal existence." Few people around me seem to be in this perpetual state of vigilance, which is why I think often that I am an unnecessary burden to those around me. If I was not here, they wouldn't need to make allowances for my sh*t in their own lives.

I recently learned that some people don't have a mind's eye, that the constant, multiple narratives and mental images that don't and can't have words that play in my head all day is not a universal trait. When there aren't yet words, I see pictures and colors and these amorphous ideas like large clouds imploding and exploding constantly until a picture takes form that filters into a description that words can contain. I can't imagine living without this "movie reel," yet I can't help but feel a bit jealous of those who have mental peace.

I once had a conversation with a client where he was asking for my expertise, but what he really wanted to do was for me to agree with him and just do what he wanted. I can respect a client who says, "I want to do this thing this way and I just need you to implement it." It happens a lot and mostly, on the small things—like using this headshot over that one, this color over that—but in this particular case, the feature in question was one that would become harmful to his brand over time. I explained what and why. He hung onto his opinions. I tried another approach and still, he hung on.

"Why," I asked? After all, he hired me to be the expert. In the end, we compromised.

I knew I was being difficult, but it was for his benefit. Perhaps he didn't see it that way because after we said goodbye and in that moment before each clicked our respective "hang up" buttons on the phones, I heard him scream, "JESUS F*CKING CHRIST!"

He perhaps was unaware his circuit was still open.

That has stuck with me for over a decade.

Was I being too obstinate? Maybe, but if I just did what he wanted me to do without push-back, his life surely would have been easier that day, even if it would have gone badly further on down the road.

I feel most people are nice to me just to get what they want. Once they get what they want from me, I am disposable. If they don't get what they want from me, someone else will do just as well. I'm merely a battery that fuels them. When they have used me up, I am tossed aside.

I recently read from a local publisher that she gets pitched memoirs mostly by middle-aged white men, close to 90% of all pitches. She doesn't even read them as the market is already over-saturated and nobody buys them unless you are super famous. And even then, it's a gamble.

There are approximately 20.5 million men between the ages of 55-65 in the United States. About 73% of these are white, giving us about 14.9M middle-aged white men. Not a day goes by when I'm not reminded in some media channel that I am a member of the most disposable, useless and unwanted population alive. Nobody wants to publish our stories or even hear that we are aware of our own disposability and redundancy. Even this screed you are reading now has already garnered eight-two thousand eye-rolls and forty-seven thousand, six hundred and twelve deep sighs.

When we were younger men, we were expected to be silent, stoic and unemotional as we bore the weight of the primary provider of familial income, food and shelter. Now that we have time and space to tell our stories, nobody wants to hear them. The appetite for us has been satiated. The narrative of us has already been written by those with more authority.

There goes another eye-roll. I heard it.

Contrary to popular media narratives, the majority of us middle-aged white men don't have powerful jobs. The majority of us have been worked beyond usability and economic viability, saddled with outdated skills and dated ideas, rendering us in physical and emotional pain, simply waiting to die. Repairing or retraining us is an investment with negative returns, so nobody is interested.

We're also very lonely, having few if any friends. A lover or primary companion has long since tired of us and few are willing to take us on, fearing an overwhelming emotional burden. It's just as well because we are mostly skittish about the expectations you have that we won't be able to fulfill.

I'd tell you this, but you don't want to hear it. Instead, I'll avoid you, change the subject if a conversation becomes too personal, keep you on read and ghost you at my earliest opportunity, perhaps leaving you confused when you should be grateful I spared you the mess roiling under these green eyes and gray hair. It would only get worse for you as I age; a look that is simply a resignation of mortality and a wasted life. It too, is a lie.

Your youth need not be wasted on those who wasted theirs.

As I was saying earlier before we got off on a side track in the middle of nowhere without a handcar, we both survived the pandemic so far. But we won't survive life. It doesn't matter when or where we exit; it's always going to be in the middle of something more important going on, probably inconvenient to someone. Life will go on; the faster the better.

I've been everywhere I wanna go; seen everything I wanna see... I'm tired of being me — *Flack* on Amazon Prime

I first said something similar to my optometrist about ten years back, when she said I will probably need cataract surgery in my lifetime. I replied I didn't mind going blind, that I'd seen everything I really wanted to see. She started to tear up like that was the saddest thing she'd ever hear. I assured her I was at peace and she should be as well. It's irrational to strive to see and do everything.

A person can only experience so much in a life.

It would be best if you each carried on as if I never existed.

---

*To be clear about one thing; I don't believe god exists. The title of this essay is one hundred percent click bait based on common parlance use in the culture. Seriously, I'm not up for that debate on anything relating to a god. Believe what you want; leave me out of it.

18

ON CHANGE

Mårup Kirke is a small church outside of the town of Lønstrup on the far northwest coast of Denmark overlooking the North Sea. Since 1250 until 2008, it sat silently weathering the winds of northern Denmark and defying the erosion of the North Sea.

In 1808, a British frigate on its way from England to Gothenburg, Sweden sank in the North Sea off the coast of Denmark. The people of the parish buried the dead in a common grave next to Mårup Kirke.

Today, you can stand on the edge of the graveyard overlooking the North Sea—which used to be its center—lean over the edge, look at the face of the cliff and see bones sticking out.

I was last at Mårup Kirke in July 2007 with my good friend Peter. It would be my last opportunity to visit the church before the kommune started dismantling it and putting it in storage. Like any good American, I remarked that it was sad that the cliffs were eroding, the church would not be there for future generations and the stories of the men buried there would just be washed out to sea.

And like any good Dane, he just shrugged and said, "Well, the coast is eroding here on the west, but it's building up in the east. Pretty soon, we'll be able to walk to Sweden."

19

A SMALL LIFE

When I was young, I dreamed of living a large life. My world then was a neighborhood—Frogtown in St. Paul, to be exact. We had three blocks down to the Victoria Hill, two blocks over to West Minnehaha Park and when we were older, hopped over the fence to the BN railroad tracks and walked the three miles to Kmart. There was Thomas and Dale to the Diebel Drug Store. Across from that drug store was the Speedy Market and down the street was St. Agnes Church and the school I went to for 13 years.

A little further on Dale was University which led to the library on Lexington and Ax-Man Surplus, a glorious playground of everything old, reeking of dust, grease and sweat. But we had to cross in front of some crack houses to get there, even though crack wasn't really a thing then. Coke, smack, snow; whatever you called it and scarier drugs that needed needles. If we got past those houses without being harassed, there were the hookers outside the Belmont and the 25¢ peep show houses to cross, but once we got to the bakery with the best doughnuts in St. Paul, we were safe. Nobody bothered kids on University between St. Albans and Snelling. We had no money and the fight wasn't worth the grab.

Man, I wanted out.

When I was nine years old, I got three paper routes when St. Paul had two newspapers, the Pioneer Press and the Dispatch. Every day, I was up at 4:00am to deliver the papers before school, then home in the afternoon to deliver the Dispatch. Every day for five years. No days off, no weather too bad to skip.

That's how you knew which kids were poor back then. The kids with the paper routes had a little spending money for the drug store, but could never take a day off. My family couldn't afford a vacation and the most we ever went anywhere was Lake Gervais in the summertime.

My world was small, but I raged every day. I didn't want to deliver the newspaper, I wanted to write for it. I didn't want to slog through manual labor, I wanted to be paid for a thinking job. I saved my money for college and a car. Up and out, that's where I was going.

The pandemic made my life small again. It's still small.

Some days, I like it in my cocoon. I should be satisfied with what I have, that this is all there is and I should be happy with who I am and what I've done. I have a house, an income for now, a dog that walks with me every afternoon, though she is now fourteen and I'm not sure how long that will last.

I'm getting old now and things cross my mind at the oddest moments, like how easily America throws away its older people because it is a place where the only use for a human body is to make money for someone else. When you can no longer do that easily, you are discarded like a piece of worn machinery.

I'm not whining, I'm just stating an empirical, observable fact.

Or how I have spent my entire life making life frictionless for others and realize now too late that I have not done what I wanted without compromise. Not entirely what I wanted, just somewhere in the comfortable middle which almost always seemed to be the exact thing others wanted for themselves, but tolerable for me. It was still in the zone, so I relented.

I can always tell when I voice a dream too far out of the comfort zone of others. They get really quiet, perhaps fearful that I will actually do it.

IT'S JUST TOO late to live a larger life without being marked as a difficult person, perhaps even one who abandons friends and family for selfish pursuits. Nobody ever remembers how you made their life frictionless. Or how much money you made them.

Most weekends, I wallow in the sad. Joy is a luxury I can't afford.

I think often that statistically, I have less than a decade to live, fewer than ten years. That's roughly about ten more Christmases. I love Christmas, but with the exception of one a little over two decades ago, I have had to celebrate the Christmas everyone else wanted. I nod, I smile and say "thank you" at the gifts, I show up when and where I'm told. I put up the tree every year, but every year, it's always decorated not quite right, not shaped quite right, the lights are all wrong.

Maybe next year I'll get it right and not have to apologize for screwing up the holiday.

I'm not "anything." I'm not a doctor, lawyer, plumber, teacher, roofer, accountant. I'm just ... a big mess who did whatever job paid the bills best. Now, I'm just a shell of a small life. No, it's true, so if your inclination right now is to disagree with me, that you see me as more than what I see myself, please stop. I am a small person in a small place doing small things. And when all my Christmases have expired, I'll be a small blimp in a memory somewhere for a very small amount of time.

I draw the shades and nobody knows I'm here, though they watch me walk my dog in the middle of the afternoon. One day, I won't walk and the next, they might look in on me.

But I won't be here.

The only thing now keeping me to this small life is knowing nobody else will walk the dog. When she goes, so will I.

20

A DEAD SQUIRREL

I stood on my front porch as flurries fell in the early morning, staring across the street in the dark at a dead squirrel under the tree in my neighbors yard, waiting for my old dog to decide to join me for a walk. The squirrel had died almost two weeks ago, but it was cold then and she had frozen under the snow. Then it got warm and she changed from a serene slumber to a grotesquely bloated blob. Soon, she will be part of the earth and then, gone. You'll care more about a dead squirrel in your front yard than people dying in Africa, he said. But he was wrong.

My dog is very old and will soon die. I will also soon die. We will both also eventually be gone.

I thought about birds and cows and how each of these creatures decide they don't want to die, that they fight against the dying of the light, at how each of their lives have been decided by human experts who want to feel better about killing animals to not be a choice, but an instinct. Animals that aren't human don't make choices, we're told, they live by instinct.

Only I know my dog decides when she wants to go on a walk. I know she chooses which direction to go, where to sniff, whether or not she wants me to scratch her ears. I know she chooses which other dogs and humans and bovines and felines she likes and who she won't be friends with. It stretches credulity to believe these things are mere instinct.

I don't know what powers each of us, from the smallest spider to the biggest human. We each have a life source that doesn't need batteries that's powered by what the earth provides in water and air and nutrients that also regenerates. We gather data from our senses and know the color blue is magnificent without knowing why, but some of us spend our entire lives trying to figure it out, knowing in our hearts we will never really know. We don't need to reboot or recharge and only have one dead state from which we don't recover.

We don't need data crammed into us to understand the world around us. Our intelligences are not artificial but are interconnected with every other part of nature and every other life, and it powers our own whether or not we are aware.

Like how the dead squirrel is pulling at me from the front as I wait for my old dog to push her nose through the screen door behind me. I can feel her getting up from the sofa as I write this, as you can as you read it. These few words connect us together, maybe for a few seconds, perhaps for the rest of our lives whenever each of us thinks about a dead squirrel or an old dog.

We are in a constant state of powered up, from the first breath to the last, every day in between, even when we sleep. Staring out through the falling snow, into the pre-dawn darkness at the dead squirrel I couldn't see but knew was there, its waning force I could feel in my own soul, I thought about all these lives all at once, those billions and billions of lives all cranking away because of a force we knew was powering them but don't really understand, and the millions dying off the same time millions were raging into being with their first breath or intake of whatever gives them life, it was all too overwhelming and I felt tears leak out of my eyes and freeze to my cheeks.

I do care about people dying in Africa. I do care about the dead squirrel across the street in my neighbor's front yard. I care about each equally as they were each drawn from the same life force that we all share.

21

59 1/2 YEARS

Warning: *Ideation theme below. If this is a trigger for you, proceed with caution or stop reading, whatever you need to do to stay safe.*

"59 1/2 YEARS. That's enough."

That's what the hand-written note said when they discovered her a week or so after she scribbled it out, a cord around her neck, the other end attached to the plumbing. It's a marker that lives in my head every day, something to gauge myself against.

"59 years, six months and I'm still here. I'm doing ok."

"59 years, six months, one day and I'm still here. I'm doing ok."

"59 years, six months, two days and ..."

I've done this calculation almost every day since she was discovered. Over and over, it pops up randomly in my head. I'm well past that 59 1/2 point—into my 60s now—but not by enough where the memory of it has faded. I still calculate almost every day.

She was the first "solid" family friend we made since moving from Minneapolis, unlike the party crowd down my street. She had three kids, was married to a boring, inattentive man with a stable government job, bought a house in a cul-de-sac and was curious about the world. She had an "almost" college degree and was a voracious reader. She had strong opinions on pretty much everything and was the first to start researching what she didn't know. Old school style researching. The kind where you go to the library and take out books, journals and periodicals. She hated tech and wouldn't text or receive texts from anyone.

"59 1/2 years. That's enough."

Her dad was abusive and her mom was controlling. She lost both too late in life. Her siblings didn't like her all that much because she would challenge their conservative beliefs. She was an atheist and could argue religion with anyone because that's what being raised Catholic does for you; a deep understanding of the tenets of faith and an unbreakable bond with atheism.

She could not cook but loved having a huge Thanksgiving and Christmas dinner at her house. I would get up at 4am, prep all the food at her house, start the turkey and go back home, coming and going back and forth from my house to hers when things needed to be rotated in and out of oven. Her house was just one subdivision over, so it was a nice walk.

Dinner with both families was a big, noisy affair.

"59 1/2 years. That's enough."

Eventually, her kids all left, one by one as kids do. Her home fell quiet and lonely. The marriage fell apart and she bought a cute little house into the city with the settlement money. My kids also grew up and out, so it was a bit easy to lose that frequent touch

---

When they were cleaning up after her departure, another note was found, unopened, slid through the mail slot in the door. She had not "healed" from trauma the way her kids thought she should and they told her.

But she had already arrived at that conclusion in her own time, in her own way.

22

RUSTING AWAY

THINK BACK TEN YEARS. Does it feel like just yesterday or does it feel like a lifetime ago? Your answer will likely depend on how old you are.

I have friends across every generation. I think most people with healthy friendships do, though I'm not claiming health. The only real issue is there are things I don't get invited to, like music festivals in the woods that my younger friends attend or bingo tournaments that my older friends frequent. But there are enough friends closer to both sides of my age that I get invited to enough things.

Most of my friends who have died lately were in the ages I will become in the next decade than I was in the past. This is sobering and if I'm being honest like a good friend would be, it's a bit panic-inducing.

I'm not afraid to die because I've already died once. One minute I was talking and laughing with the living and the next, I realized I had no choice and resigned to the sleep. There is that moment right before you know you'll be dead where you'll feel a limitless, indescribable calm. Just let go, fall like Seth in the movie, *City of Angels*.

Dying is more dramatic and terrifying for the living, but to die, that's pretty easy to do. What most of us don't want to do is the process of dying, the rusting away.

I had no process. One minute, I was in the IVIG center, chatting with the Friday regulars and the next, I realize I'm going to die and then... I'm dead. Obviously, the medical staff brought me back to life or I wouldn't be writing this right now but I quit breathing, I had no pulse.

I'll never forget the face of my oncology nurse when I opened my eyes. She was scared and nervous and relieved, then she got mad at me for dying on her watch. Her eyes welled up and she walked away because apparently a patient is not supposed to see his nurse cry.

I spend a fair amount of time dreading the unknown. I spend even more time dreading the predictable known. I pace, I eat, I walk the subdivision at the Devil's Hour.

Every future event that can be predicted falls into two categories; those with hard deadlines and those without a deadline. I know I am going to die, but I don't know when. I know my laptop and servers will cycle out of date, but I don't know when. I know my car will break down, I know my fridge will quit running, though the latter is more certain than the former.

I know my dog will die, but I don't know when. She's got some nerve issues and frequently loses her balance. It happens more frequently lately.

Me and my dog, we're no longer dying; we're rusting away.

23

THE VALUE OF OLD MEN

Old men are a dime a dozen and worth less than my .02

I spend more time than I should on TikTok and even more time on the other socials. The overwhelming opinion about older men on all platforms is we are ruining the world with our archaic point of view.

But the truth is far more nuanced than that. In the first place, we exist in fewer numbers[1] than older women. We don't have a union or a community[2] regardless of how our popular media and influencer women want to portray us. We don't roam in packs and we're mostly loners. We die sooner than women. The vast majority of us have no political, social or economic power.

Old men are only valued by our culture if they are able to fuel the ambitions of the young.

The few loudmouths you do see abusing power are so rare that they suck up all the oxygen, giving media personalities and influencers fuel to point to them as representative of us all.

If you've come here to affirm that older men are role models for young boys on how to be a man, I'm gonna

---

1. Of course I researched this. Do you think I just pull numbers out of my butt? Men outpace women slightly until about 45 where the drop-off is significant and accelerated. Men just die earlier.
2. The local Dunkin' doesn't count. It doesn't. That's just hospice without the morphine and co-pays. (For my non-American readers, co-pay is the money you have to spend before your over-priced medical insurance will pay for any care. If you have no money, you get no care.)

disappoint you. At one point in my life when I was a young man, I believed that.

I envied friends who had dads around when they were growing up, who had them in their lives well into middle age. Having arrived at this side of the fence, I realize those dads were always playing the character of someone else; even as they lay breathing their last, they were a character in someone else's diorama, with well-established fences on a full electrical charge.

"Don't touch the thin wires." They might be unplugged, but you're never quite sure.

Just as it didn't matter to others what you thought or felt while living, it won't matter as you lay dying.

"Go quietly, as un-opinionated as you lived." Nobody is listening and fewer still are writing it down. There's very little point in saying any last words.

Most of us are just tired, want to be left alone and die quietly with little to no fuss. We've lived a life of not living up to anyone's expectations, including our own. At some point, we realized we were just excess baggage in everyone else's life, a convenient excuse for their own failures and dying dreams.

24

THE PATRIARCH

A YOUNG MALE friend of mine—in his mid 30s—responded in a text thread recently that I was the Patriarch in my family. I think I knew what he meant, but I still recoiled at the word. Since then, the idea of a male hierarchy has been rolling around in my noggin as I desperately try to reject the notion as not a thing, even though it clearly lives in our culture.

I don't wanna be the Patriarch.

Did that sound like I was whining and stomping my feet, maybe holding my breath like little Bobbie in a toy store who isn't getting a toy he wants? If so, I think we understand each other about older male expectations. I can't do that in our culture. "Man up," you might have said internally.

Good. We're on the same page. Let's have a conversation.

I'm thinking on how mostly younger wyte dudes can't quite adapt to the newer realities of masculinity, i.e., what it means to be a man. I've read Bell Hooks' *The Will to Change* three times so far, trying to wrap my head around a singular thesis that explains what is going on. It's not just a simple "old wyte dudes" or "Patriarchy," even though that does factor in. Hooks has it in the book but it's complicated and hard to distill into one sentence or paragraph.

I come across an article in "History Today" June 2023 and this quote:[1]

> As history progresses, political, social and economic circumstances change. The powerful of one era are not the same as those of the preceding one, even when they are their lineal descendants.

I think this might just all boil down to some sort of inheritance expectation men have at every stage of their lives; boys, teens, young men, men, fathers, grandfathers, elders and they see it not only being taken from them, but violently ripped from them.

Clearly, it is more perception than reality ... or maybe not ... but the idea that there are "winners" in some sort of gender war or that there is a gender war at all is a bit problematic and sad. A narrative built on perception is mostly going to win out over facts, frustrating—and employing—historians everywhere.

Even the way they see themselves "losing" this "inheritance"—violently, at the hands of an enemy and in zero sum fashion—supports the Patriarchy.

Of course, like every essay I publish, this thought is incomplete and might be wrong

My personal interest in this is I have a son (39) and two grandsons (4 & 3, six months apart.) I recently told a generational peer friend of mine, who is also a granddad, the most wisdom we can pass down is to listen and nod a lot; I don't want to be the Patriarch; I don't want to drive anything anymore.

This was immediately disputed by my granddad friend who believes the elders should be imparting knowledge and wisdom. I'm not so sure the "funnel" into the younger generations is like it was when I was growing up. (I didn't grow up having any of this stuff which may have just been a middle class narrative that wasn't really true for a lot of us, but I digress)

This friend is hanging onto the expectation that he was promised he would be respected and revered when

---

1. https://www.historytoday.com/archive/head-head/history-written-winners

he reached a certain age, but I don't think that is true today when anything can be looked up on the internet. We both "gentlemen of a certain age" did not have the internet, but we did have older people with experience. Today, we are no longer the gatekeepers of knowledge, know-how and wisdom.

I think the role of older men is changing to be listeners and nodders, maybe a gentle nudge away from dangerous thoughts like ... "should I vote Republican" or "should I join that militia" ... but for the most part, talk less, listen more.

My generational peer friend is really struggling with being "useless" because of this expectation he feels others have of him and he has of himself. He thinks I'm daft because listening and nodding, in his world, is doing a whole lot of nothing. I also fear that by listening and nodding, I'm perpetuating a stereotype of men not talking about what they are thinking. Yet, I try to be conscious of starting off a conversation with my son with some form of, "do you want me to listen, give advice or solve a problem?"

Thoughts?

Ahhhhh... you're listening and nodding, ain't ya?

25

YOUR DOG DOESN'T KNOW YOU ARE MENTALLY UNSTABLE

IF YOUR DOG knew just how close you were to jumping off the planet, would she still rely on you for walks and her dinner every day. Would she still sleep so close to you without fear?

If she knew how many times a day you thought about leaving, would she split and seek out more security for herself or would she stay and hold you?

Does she feel the unease, the constant anxiety and if so, does she think it's the normal state of being?

I read a newsletter I subscribe to this morning and it speaks to the bravery of loving someone. I'm not sure I agree with the author, but I'm not going to say it publicly in the comments. I think loving someone when you are thinking of leaving is selfish; when you leave them, you won't feel the pain of loss, but they will. It's kinder to not connect with them, to let them go so they don't miss you when you're not there, even if the band-aid rip hurt.

I also recently saw† a series of TikToks and articles about how WFH is destroying our "Third Places." I realized I had worked from home for almost fifteen years now, with my Third Place being the park, the lake, the forest with the dog pack being down to just one geriatric dog for whom walking up a ramp and riding in a van for the 5–10 minutes to the "Third Place" is painful. Expecting her to walk around the lake or through a wooded path would just be cruel.

I realized last week that I had unwittingly relied on social media spaces like LinkedIn as my Third Space. The danger of LinkedIn being a Third Space is you create relationships with very real people. You can't just go there and sit quietly with a book, a cup of coffee, a walk with a dog. You get to know people and they know you.

The panic this realization created was overwhelming and embarrassing when I let it happen; embarrassing because that Third Place became more real than my second and first place. That Third Place was me being who I couldn't in my first and second.

I realized also that LinkedIn could never find me the two things I desperately need in my life. One of these things is a job, a second space, a place to go every day where I am needed and wanted. Never mind what the other thing is; we're not that close and never will be.

Does my talking frankly about this topic make you uncomfortable? Does it make you want to reach out, to make sure I am ok? Please don't. Unlike a lot of other writers, I don't want to know you are there, reading my words, poking at the folds of my brain, fingering my ribs to get to my heart.

I work hard at staying in character in every space of my life and I don't want you in the room I am in. You can peer into the windows, listen with your ear to the door; I don't want to know. Trust me when I say the idea of a relationship with me is a lot safer than an actual relationship with me. You don't want to get close.

I don't have a writerly contempt for you, I truly don't. I'm just not that mean. It's when I know you are looking, I get all flustered and stutter. I see myself as one way in my mind that any ordinary mirror belies. I close my eyes when I play music on a stage; I imagine myself differently when I write and I need to maintain that same illusion as you read this. Writing out essays, publishing them out there—*spins around slowly with arms outstretched, head thrown back*—is my way of thinking all of these complex feeling through, the balance between sanity and insanity, life and death, love and indifference.

Let's go back to the dog, where feelings are clear, thought is lucid.

The logical thing for the dog to do would be to jump ship, find another human that will provide for her needs. If she continues to hold onto someone who will leave her or can no longer support her, she will die of starvation, disease or exposure. Being loyal to me because of love is irrational, a death sentence.

Yet, she is here and has no contingency plan.

Living with a dog is like explaining gravity on a micro-scale. Proximity to her keeps me alive as proximity to me keeps her alive. As long as we both exist, we can't pull away too far without being pulled back to each other. But the reality is one of us is eventually going to have to live without the other. Common wisdom says I'll say goodbye to her rather than her to me, but that is not guaranteed.

A dog dealing with the pain of grief is heartbreaking because they live in the same moment, over and over, without knowing the grief will eventually end. It's enough heartbreak to keep me holding on. If she leaves me first, I won't grieve for long as I'll be following her.

Because ... gravity.

---

† No, I did not save any of the links. I want to get better at this. I did not link to anything, but you are free to dig around what I read here and follow along in those spaces. You're the boss of you! There might be typos and weird editing... I wrote most of this on cold walks around the neighborhood while my old dog was resting.

26

MY NEIGHBORHOOD DIED

I walk my last remaining dog down the street and back every morning, passing the house where Tammy and her son, her husband and his brother and her sister lived. Across the street is the house where Ged and his wife Carol lived. They had two young kids. This was the nerve center of life when we first moved into the neighborhood, two houses down. A few houses the other way, lived a large family of five kids, a couple more down, a new young couple with two girls would move in a year after we did. Across the backyard, my daughter would stand at the fence with a toddler who became her best friend for a while. That toddler is now a mom of triplets and her dad, one of my last neighbor friends who knew how to do anything, died last Christmas.

Carol got cancer and died. Ged died a few years ago from the bottle. Tammy moved away and I sometimes hear from her when life gets too boring. Her sister died this past summer. A sad dad and his son he sees once a month moved into Ged and Carol's house. Everyone except me has moved on and away. The neighborhood became quiet for a while as the housing crisis took a few more families away, the elements weathered even more as cash dried up.

And I stayed.

I should have moved on as well when the neighborhood shifted, but I needed a stable base to weather a pretty big medical thing. My kids had grown and flown, the older graduated with a BFA, tearing up the restaurant scene in NYC, the younger in her last two years of college.

I'm now the old man in that one house who walks his dog every day. "That dog is so old," the kids probably murmur to each other as the school bus passes every morning. Eventually, my dog will die, probably soon. Her back legs have failed her more than a few times already.

New families have moved into the houses the young families of my youth once lived in, but they are not the same. We wave to each other as one would wave to a neighborhood regular they see every day, but I have not been invited inside. I know the children and have watched them grow. They pet my dog. five years is nothing to an old man, but five years is half their lifetime. five more is a whole lifetime.

Ten years is a blink of an eye to an old man, a shoebox of filed memories and a closet full of ghosts.

But my mirror sees the aging and my head tells me that I should move on. But my heart is not quite ready to leave this home.

One more year. One more year.

27

IT'S ABOUT TIME

THIRTY YEARS and eleven days ago[1], I moved to Englewood, Ohio from Minneapolis, Minnesota. In those thirty years, I have attended parades and watched foot races along Union and National, but I have never participated in or attended a political protest in those streets. It wasn't because I was unwilling or inactive; it was because a protest has never happened here.

Yesterday, we broke that streak when several hundred people showed up to march at 5:11pm, protest and rally in our little city of 13,000 and ten miles north of Dayton, Ohio for racial justice and equality.

It was about time.

The protestors marched from Centennial Park on Union, down National to the Englewood Government Center where speakers delivered a message and knelt for eight minutes and forty-six seconds. While the protest comprised people of diverse races, genders and ages, the organizers and speakers were young and Black.

Police officers from Brookville, Clayton and Butler County came to help the Englewood police control the counter-protestors? (one dude with a thin blue line flag and another parked in his pickup truck next to me filming it all) stop the folks from rioting and looting? (there was an abandoned Kmart across the street. The City zoning ordinances have done more to create blight than any rioters could) break up the crowd that refused

---

1. This essay was originally written on June 12, 2020.

to leave? (folks dispersed quietly and peacefully at 5:42pm when they said what they needed to say.)

I don't really know what the police were expecting, but mostly they just put out traffic cones across the intersections so the protestors could march peacefully, assemble and rally at the City Center while keeping the white folks who got themselves trapped in the old Kmart parking lot—because they couldn't read the huge signs about the streets being closed—from leaving the lot while running over cones and... I dunno, people and puppies?

Anyway, there were more cops than anyone needed to control a riot that never happened in a city that has never seen a protest. Maybe they were really there to assure the white people that they were going to be safe and protected.

We'll get better at it in time.

Englewood, Ohio on June 12, 2020. Photo by Gerard Mclean
#BlackLivesMatter

28

THE FLOWER AND THE DIRT

Here's what I know about activism:

I've been a rabble rouser for more than half a century. It's hard to get people to follow, even though you are leading in the right direction. Change, social pressures, fear of losing income, whatever... it's just hard. I get it.

But you keep going; you do the small things[1]. One day at a time, one foot in front of the other.

Then something horrible happens like #SandyHook or #floridaSchoolShooting or #Ferguson that is in your realm of activism, that you've been putting in time and sweat and heart. Some folks rise up and get celebrity like @deray and @Nettaaaaaaaa and now @delaneytarr @cameron_kasky @davidhogg111 @Emma4Change @NeverAgainMSD (follow them on twitter and other social spaces.)

Not gonna lie here, the first human reaction is getting pissed off and thinking "I've been doing the work forever" "WHAT ABOUT ME??!"

But, yeah, what about you? Why do you need credit

---

1. One of the small things I did was protest the IraqWar, but not in the way you'd think. I was at the DDN at the time and there was a "Wear Red, White and Blue Day" ... to "support the troops." I wore a yellow shirt and blue jeans. Those who were in editorial knew the message I was sending them. I hope they felt some shame. The rest thought I was not a team player and they were right; not on that team. I knew the IraqWar for what it was. Simple acts of defiance; they get under the skin of those who enforce status quo. Think harder.

for the work you did? Why does your ego matter more than the mission?

It doesn't.

It's an instinctive reaction but not the mature one. Pound the desk if you need to, then focus on those who are getting the attention and ask, "How can I help?" Stow the ego and get behind those who have emerged as leaders. Don't splinter off the efforts of the mission. Pay forward. Everything you do is paying forward.

Sometimes you're the dirt and sometimes you're the flower. Have the emotional and mental maturity to know which you are in this fight. Understand each needs the other. #NeverAgain #NeverAgain #NeverAgain If even one more life is saved at the cost of my ego, it's worth the price.

Sponsor a student if you can.

29

MY LETTER TO MARC LACEY AT THE NEW YORK TIMES

December 1, 2017

Marc Lacey
National Editor
The New York Times
620 Eighth Avenue
New York, NY 10018

Mr Lacey;

I've read the article "A Voice of Hate in America's Heartland" and your response to the reaction, mostly on social media. While I share the concern about normalizing Nazis, this letter is not that.

I hope I have kept you reading beyond this point. I believe by the end of my letter, you may have a different point of view about Ohio. At least that is my goal in writing to you.

I get it. I live just down the road from Huber Heights, here amongst the deep pool of unsophisticated rubes, hicks, hillbillies and hobos that make up most of Southwest and Appalachian Ohio. It is easy as a national newspaper to dip into that pool and pull out a great story —or two, or three or more—that paints a picture of the hollowing out of The Middle. You don't have to wade deep into it to find someone with little education, a gun, a Bible and a racist dream. In my subdivision alone, I can easily find half a dozen houses flying the Gadsden's flag.

I'm a transplant to Ohio, having moved here in 1991 from Minneapolis for a job at Huffy Corporation, a Fortune 500 company long since sold off for parts. I view my transplantation as an advantage, with the ability to look out into this area of Ohio with an objective eye, untainted by a culture that the natives wear as "normal."

Allow me to share with you just a small sliver of what I see in Ohio.

Ohioans invented the car starter, the hot dog, Teflon, rubber, the vacuum cleaner, the pop-top can, the cash register, and most famously, Ohio invented controlled powered flight.[1]

Every time an airplane takes off and lands at LGA, JFK or any other airport around the world, Ohio made that happen. Every time you hear a car engine roar to life, Ohio did that. Every time you hear someone pop open a cold beer on a hot day, Ohio did that. Every time you hear a cash register ding, see a swipe across an app, a payment transaction in a coffee shop or bodega, Ohio did that.

In short, Ohio—specifically Dayton—invented most of the modern world you and I now take for granted. Ohio has also produced eight presidents for the United States of America.

Where others may see unsophisticated madness, I see the scrappiness necessary to produce ideas the world has not yet discovered it needs. I think of today's Ohio not as a pool of nutjobs, but as a sleeping giant, with incredibly smart and creative people impatient for the world to catch up. The ashes of the industrial ruins that blanket our state are fertilizing and growing young

---

1. The list is far longer, but this is a print letter and column inches are expensive. Hey, I'm an old ink-stained newsie and I had to at least try to end on a newspaper joke.

PS: They say the easiest way to learn a foreign language is to immerse yourself entirely in the foreign country where learning to speak the language means the difference between living and starving to death. Use that nugget of wisdom and immerse a journalist or two in Ohio. I've got two spare bedrooms and would love the company, the intellectual conversations in the evenings, the off-the-record banter in the wee hours of the morning around a kitchen table. Heck, "My Year in Ohio" could even be a story; just spit-balling here, not pitching.

But seriously, I've got two spare rooms. Must love dogs.

shoots that will eventually grow into mighty stalks, titans of the industries of which they are now only babes.

Those are the stories of Ohio I encourage you to seek out and write. It took the *Dayton Daily News* an entire century to finally discover the contributions of Orville and Wilbur Wright. The journalists at the *News* and *Journal* laughed at these two idiots and their flying contraption. By 2003, Dayton, Ohio had lost its legacy, having been claimed by Kitty Hawk, North Carolina, who saw greatness and potential where others only saw crazy.

I encourage the journalists at the *New York Times* to learn from the mistakes of their c. 1903 peers at the *News* and *Journal*. Don't do the easy, obvious story. Dig deeper into the whys and hows and seek to understand the history of how that one subject got to that one moment in time that the journalist is now witnessing. Then seek to understand further by imagining the trajectory of time into the future and the intended and unintended consequences the subject will bring to bear. Use the human intuition, fear and hope that journalists suppress to shape the human story for human beings.

It may not be what journalists are taught in J-School. In fact, I know it is not; but it is the skill set that is now required in today's modern journalism where every eyeball—informed, sophisticated or not—is trained on every word they write. You can either fight this or embrace this as the new journalism reality.

And give us in Ohio a break. We're not all gun-toting, Nazi-loving, Bible-thumping nutbags.

Regards,

Gerard McLean

30

WHAT DO YOU NOT WRITE ABOUT?

Not a day goes by when I don't read some essay about someone who is or wants to be a writer, bemoaning the fact that they don't know what to write about, the well has gone dry, the creative spark has extinguished.

What do I write about? Give me a prompt, show me the way...

I can't identify with this because my head is constantly and forever writing prose. I write narratives in my head of me in the third person, looking at me doing something banal, like walking up a flight of stairs, sitting on a park bench, staring at a piece of wrought iron railing. Sometimes I throw these things away, sometimes I throw them online and sometimes I tuck them away in my head, in my own private little vault.

But I never have nothing to write about; quite the opposite—I have too much.

To always know what to write, to write better, see the world around you. See yourself. See others.

See the way her hair twirls around her neck, how her nose turns up slightly on her profile, how her cheeks and lips purse when she thinks a thought she dare not say. Look into her eyes and see the soul that aches for a moment of rest, prone against your open thigh, but dare not ask for it.

See yourself seeing her and how she sees you. How would you write that? Would you toss that away or tuck it into your head where nobody but you will read it? Or will you share small bits online just in case she sees it?

See. Feel. Write.
Find the words.

THE POETRY OF JOURNALISM

My short article wireframe poetry for writing a piece of journalism:

Hed, Dek, Lede.
Graf Graf Graf
Kicker.

The words are not misspelled either. That really is ink-stained wretchedness.

I teach this "poem" to anyone looking to write blog posts or engage in journalism. Articles and posts longer or more complicated than this don't get read.

Copy it, frame it, post it on a wall, live it. Make your stories conform.

Hed: Headline, write this last.

Dek: That little piece of fluff that Google likes on the link, right under the hed. This is your tease pitch. Write it after everything else has been written. If you have an editor, copyeditor, best friend, loyal dog, it's best if they read your piece without you in the room and write the dek in their own words. Do not exceed 160 characters or your story is dead.

Lede: first "graf" or paragraph of the story. Get your 5Ws in there and get them hitting hard. You don't want anyone leaving your lede without knowing what the hell you are talking about. Ironically, about 2/3rds of your readers will click off after your lede, either confused or smug with the false knowledge of knowing what you are writing.

Graf: A paragraph that expands on the lede and leads to the kicker. You get three hits in any one story; make them count. Graf, Graf, Graf. Say it fast and hard. Graf! Graf! Graf! Write the same way. Dig in and don't let up.

Kicker: Write this first. Write the grafs, then make sure you pull up on the throttle. Link back the first sentence in the kicker to the last sentence in the lede. If you can't, keeping working the story until you can.

Tight, tight, tight. Then tighten it even more. Question every adverb, interrogate every adjective. Seriously, do you really need to introduce a graf with a conjunction? Knock that sh*t off.

Now shut off the screen you are staring at and go do something worth writing about.

32

THE CORN AND THE CARROT

I WAS GOING through a pile of stuff from my corporate days, old planners, files, etc. stuffed in file boxes in my basement, stuff I would eventually get to, shred what needs shredding and throw away what doesn't fit in the slot, when I came across an old Franklin planner. I almost just tossed it when I figured I'd unzip it and see if there was anything interesting inside.

Just as I was about to toss it into the trash, a corner of a piece of paper, tucked onto the inside flap, caught my eye. I pulled it out and it was an illustrated storybook my daughter had written when she was in the fourth grade.

Affixed to the cover was a note from her teacher, which read:

Wonderful! You should get this published!

I read it and it was good. I remembered why I kept it then and I now knew what I should get her for her thirty-first birthday. It was September and her birthday was in March. I owned an imprint and knew how to publish books.

Plenty of time.

Only I had never published an illustrated children's book. I was soon in over my head. I didn't know any children's book illustrators and all my research produced illustrators whose style didn't quite capture the style I was looking for. Like every creative client, I didn't know exactly what I was looking for, but I'd felt sure I knew it when I saw it.

Turns out, I never saw it. The holidays passed by and I was running out of time.

Then one weekend, my grandkids were over and coloring with crayons in a coloring book. BAM, right over the head. That was the style I was looking for. I'd trace her drawings in black Sharpie, scale and resample to fit the square format I had decided on earlier.

After a few unsuccessful tries, I got the hang of it, selecting the consistent color palette and went to town. I had to create a couple new drawings from her existing characters to fit the page count for the printer, but it came together. Scan, correct color, place on page. Done!

Then I applied for the ISBN, LCCN ... waited for an excruciating couple of days for approval, uploaded filed to Ingram and within a couple weeks, the book was available on every online outlet as well as available for any indie bookstore to order for you and your child.

Happy birthday, Melissa! It took over twenty years for this seed to germinate, but I hope you're glad it eventually took root.

Will you autograph my copy?

The original and the published book.

33

SKOWHEGAN

A BLACK CHEVROLET, with all their belongings strapped to the roof, pulled out of Skowhegan on a frigid February pre-dawn as the snow was beginning to fall. The slapping of the worn windshield blades slowly synchronized with the soft backbeat of Johnny Horton's *Springtime in Alaska* playing from the dash radio. They had exchanged vows in the church chapel two days earlier, three days earlier he had cleared out the bank accounts, closed the hardware store and kissed his mother for the last time.

A new life lay ahead, with as much distance as he could place between then and tomorrow. He was free of the banks, free of the torment of creditors, free of the daily demands of this life. He vowed never to speak French again and not allow this vile language into his home they would make together. She was confused as it was her native language, the language that connected her with her family. He was determined to break those ties. She was his now, and a wife was obedient to her husband. The Lord said so in the Bible, the same Lord who told him in a dream to marry and flee.

This was not the man she married and it terrified her. Why did they have to leave tonight? A blizzard is rolling in.

"God will provide all that we need and clear the road for us, like Moses parted the Red Sea," he replied, wiping a tear from her face.

He saw it in a dream. She believed him; she had faith in Him.

As they crossed the state line into New Hampshire, he relaxed his shoulders and stretched his arm to invite her to him. She nuzzled into his hunter's jacket, breathed in his scent, rested her eyes and reluctantly fell asleep.

The radio began skipping from music to static and the low tones of an engine ping could be heard above the slapping blades. He scanned the airwaves for a signal, turning up the volume a bit when he found one.

34

DEAD BY FIFTY

Don't worry about marriage being forever. He'll be dead by fifty, your two kids will be adults, you'll still be young enough to date and he'll have left you a large life insurance policy.

That was the plan anyway. Too bad he lived a decade longer than planned and is showing no signs of dropping dead any time soon. He still has a full head of hair and all his teeth. Never had a heart attack and has a resting pulse rate of 69bpm, blood pressure of a 30-year old.

Oops. Now what are you gonna do?

"I can't wait to be rid of this ill-fitting meat sack I've been dragging around with me my entire life," he said, unprompted. "It's ugly, too fat in the wrong places and hurts from the inside out."

Why bother if he's gonna be dead in a few years anyway.

He is in everybody's way. It's probably time he just took the nearest off-ramp and quit causing trouble for everybody.

He suspects he spends more time wanting to be with people who would rather he not be there. The concept of spending time with loved ones assumes they also love you, but he's never sure they do. He has nothing of value they want, much less need. He is in their way, an annoyance they are forced to deal with.

His doctors write in their notes that he is angry. He reads them, almost obsessively, on his MyChart but they got it wrong. He's scared and bored and lonely, but he is not angry. He wonders if the world sees him as just another angry old man.

He fixes his face.

"When is it ok to say I've lived long enough," he muses to nobody. "Is it ever ok? What about hope... Hope for what? What if every tomorrow will be the same as today, the great expanse of nothing happening?"

Just... existence. He's told that should be enough, but it doesn't feel like that is true.

The trees are starting to bud and he has already mowed his yard once this Spring, earlier than he has ever done. He keeps records—journals of mowing dates, when those shrubs were planted, when the furnace was last repaired, when the plumbers last came out to snake the drains—because his memory has become unreliable. There are no life events to measure the mundane against anymore now that the kids have grown and flown.

Are the shrubs really fourteen years old? That can't be true; he just planted them when his daughter pulled up daily in her little truck. Has she really been gone living her life without him for that long?

Fourteen years.

Five thousand, one hundred and eighteen days of just existing. How did he endure when staring into a future of another day seems unbearable.

"What's wrong?" she asks. "Are you ok?"

"Yeah, just a little cold... thinking " he lies, wondering if she knew how deeply he was lying. If she did, she didn't let on.

He needed to either be fine or dead. The in-between was too uncomfortable to bear.

35

CANDLE FLAME

You shared your light with others.
The smoke, you saved for me.

36

MY NEUTRAL FACE

I FIRST BECAME aware of my face when I was fourteen. I had a job in a local Catholic parish rectory recording the Sunday collection plate donations and answering the phone after hours. In truth, most of the time was spent watching TV.

One evening, all the priests were together at dinner and they invited me to eat with them because it was the housekeeper/cook's day off. The menu was toast and omelettes.

I caught my reflection in the polished surface of the toaster that was sitting at the far end of the table. It didn't look anything like how I was feeling inside.

"Why do you always look so mad," she says to me often.
"I'm not mad. This is my neutral face."
"You always look so angry and that makes me mad."

I'M OFTEN giddy and awestruck by simple things. I'm amused and happy when I discover new stuff. I'm anxious and scared about others around me.

I often write long prose in my head.
But I am rarely angry. I wish my face would say that.

37

HOPE, FIRE AND DIRT

My neighbor over the backyard fence builds a fire in his home-made fire pit almost every night. I watch from my deck as he gathers sticks to use as kindling, sometimes from his own back yard, sometimes from the back compost/log/stick pile at the end of my yard within his reach.

I lend him my ladder, he burns my tree trimmings and dead wood. It keeps our world in balance. If I was being entirely honest, though, I'm mostly concerned he'll fall in because as much as he likes building fires, he also likes beer.[1]

So far, so good.

He's an old-school fire guy. He doesn't believe in using fire starter sticks or fuel accelerants, though he does use his lighter instead of a flint. He is an expert on how each kind of wood burns and how oxygen flows through a fire. He can predict how long a fire will last and how hot or brightly it will burn just by the type and age of wood he uses.

Building a roaring campfire from scratch is a painful lesson in patience. The right kindling, exact placement of the wood to invite oxygen, the careful nursing of a single spark … all these little things that must go right for the

---

1. *You might be thinking 'fire and beer' are a bad combination, but when I moved to Ohio 31 years ago, I was introduced to 'beer and drive-thru.' These folks here make it work!*

flame to catch and the logs to burn. And then there is the maintenance and vigilance so the fire doesn't go out.

But extinguishing this roaring fire is easy; just drop a clump of dirt on the flames. Done. Out. No patience needed, no planning, no concern about how to find more wood, no empathy for others who need the fire for food and warmth. Just, destruction.

Hope is the former. Hope is also what it looks like to start rebuilding a fire when someone comes along and just dumps their load of dirt on your hard work.

I'm not sure how many fires in a life each of us has within us, but as I get older and stare into the tunnel of old age in this country, I'm increasingly convinced it is one less than we each need. I want to scream at the young that hope is a trap, that there is nothing for people who hope except a Sisyphean existence of building fires.

Yet, I resist the urge to tell them to buy a shovel and a sturdy bucket. I'm beginning to feel that might be a character flaw.

38

HUSKY

Husky.

That is what they called fat kids in the '60s when politically correct took its first awkward, feeble steps. Throughout the next decade, thin enough to wear polyester pants without the pocket holes straining at the hips was the only measure of thin. Otherwise, you were husky.

Husky meant special trips to Sears because Kmart didn't carry husky. The Goodwill and the Sisters of the Poor never had husky anything. Full retail is what husky cost.

Husky meant this kid is costing more than he is worth.

"He who does not work, does not eat," my dad used to quote from the Bible often. I think it is a paraphrase and not sure which book it is from or even if it is in the Bible. Arguing it growing up would have been pointless as he applied it literally and often.

I went without supper many times in my early years for failing to do chores. I was still husky. The cure for husky, it would later prove, was a diet of cigarettes, ice water, poverty and despair.

39

BEGINNINGS

I WAS BORN in a neighborhood of St. Paul, Minnesota known as Frogtown as the second child of five to two hard-working, Catholic parents. They each grew up in Maine and were traveling to California on their honeymoon. The car broke down first in Madison, Wisconsin and then broke down for good in St. Paul. So, my dad got a job with Ingersall-Rand as a claims clerk and my mom stayed at home and made babies. As the second in a line, I did my share of baby-sitting at a very young age.

As I grew, I become more curious with the world around me, went to St. Agnes Catholic Schools for 13 years where I learned lots of life skills, discipline and a boatload of humility. This was back in the day when they still let nuns teach us poor, defenseless children. Not everyone was a winner in those days, but escaping middle school with any shred of self-esteem was considered an accomplishment worthy of a very large trophy.

In high school, we learned Latin every day, advanced algebra, sciences, English, literature and discipline... always, every day. There was no such thing as late or an excuse that would be accepted for anything. If something happened to you that you didn't get your homework done or where you didn't know the answer, it was God's way of teaching you respect and humility.

I graduated near the top of my class, but not in the top two, so I was neither the Valedictorian nor was I the

Salutatorian. These were the days when there was only one of each. Only one best per year; only one second best. I went on to study English at the University of Minnesota, mostly because that was all I could afford. I applied to and been accepted by both Harvard and USC, but these places wanted more money than I had and not being a Valedictorian or Salutatorian, they wanted me to pay the whole thing sans scholarship. I had also been accepted into the NROTC program, but at the last minute, I decided five years in the Marine Corps was probably not a good idea for either me or the Corps.

I wanted to be an English teacher or a writer. When I discovered how little they made, I decided that corporate training would be my career path of choice. With my English degree in hand, I headed off to a promising career in retail with Target Stores.

Which I did for 6 1/2 years. I didn't know it at the time, but that was the best work-prep experience I could ever have gotten. Even today, I refer to my Target days as "boot camp for the corporate world." If you can afford it, get a job at a Target store and throw yourself into it, body and soul. You will learn, you will grow.

40

BIKE GREASE

I WAS WORKING as the Area Specialist in Sporting Goods at Target during April 1987. During those days, we had a repair and assembly technician from YLCE (Yorba Linda Cycle Enterprises, before it became Huffy Service first) come in twice a week. With every visit, the tech rolled in with his cart of tools and sat in a lawn chair, reading the newspaper until I had pulled 30 or so bicycles from the back storage for him to assemble. We chatted about this and that each time and eventually got to know each other pretty well (though I can not remember his name.)

The day before he came in, I had a particularly rough tour with the district manager. For those who have never worked retail, that is when the higher-ups swoop down on your store and are hyper-critical of everything you do day to day as if that were motivation. For a demanding company like Target, *perfect* was the only standard that mattered. The previous month, they had instituted a new SKU management system and assumed everyone was on board 100%. In truth, we were still being trained on the "dot" system. But the store manager and my hardlines manager were not about to admit to the district manager that we were not at 100%. Nobody ever did.

Suffice to say, the tour went badly. And then the YLCE tech showed up, rolling in with his tools, setting up his lawn chair and reading his newspaper while I pulled bikes.

"How much do you make assembling bikes?" I asked rather casually. He told me and it was several thousand more than I was making a year. "And," he added, "I only work about six months of the year, and I get weekends and evenings off." People don't ride bikes in the winter in Minnesota.

I processed that for a few hours afterwards and figured; if I worked just 20–30% harder than this guy and scrounged around in the winter months for furniture, BBQ grills and other things to assemble and repair (YLCE was supposed to do those, but this guy just did bikes) I could make a pretty good living.

I decided I was going to quit my upwardly mobile, fast-tracked career path with Target and build bikes. I called his manager who wanted me to start tomorrow. We negotiated two weeks. I went home to tell my 19 month-old son and his mother that I was going to give up a secure job to build bikes on commission; that I had to buy my own tools with money we didn't have. As excited as I was was as terrified as she was. Fortunately I was too excited to notice or I would have chickened out.

As it turned out, I didn't even need to work 30% harder than the YLCE tech who "recruited" me into the world of self-reliance. I just needed to not sit my butt down in the chair and read a newspaper. It turns out that when you help the over-worked, under-paid retail guys pull bikes from storage, they will go the extra mile to make sure to request you and save you the best bike building days. And trust only you to do repairs.

That year, I increased my Target salary by four times. And I got weekends and holidays off. But I still worked evenings during bicycle season. Every Saturday morning that summer, I pulled my son around in a red wagon bedecked with pillows and sandbox toys as we took long walks to the post office first to mail my paperwork, to the bank to deposit my check, to the school yard to play in the sandbox, to the walkway down by the Mississippi River to watch the riversharks swim by and the French bakery to relax before heading home.

It was the best summer of my life.

41

IMPATIENT

After a couple years of care-free working, i.e., no management responsibilities, I grew anxious again for a formal leadership role. I had become the lead trainer in the Metro and had the highest trainee retention rate, all while staying at either #1 or #2 in production. But I felt I wanted more. Recognizing that perhaps I would make a good Metro/Area Manager, YLCE (now Huffy Service first) decided to split the Minneapolis Metro into two parts and give me the smaller of the two while the current metro manager would retain the other. My area extended to the MN/IA border, all of St. Paul and most of Western Wisconsin.

I spent two years exceeding sales plans, reducing turnover, and generally making my bosses in Dayton, Ohio happy. They thought that I might want to take a promotion as an Operations Training Manager at the corporate offices. It wasn't something they made easy to refuse as they had already replaced me before I said yes, so I moved to Dayton in June of 1991. My daughter had been born three months prior.

The job involved flying around the country putting on Train the Trainer workshops and various other duties that worked efficiency into all the systems that started out at the technician level and worked their way through the rest of the organization; from work orders to processing to inventory of repair parts. It was quite interesting, but as was my nature, I found myself being promoted later that year when my boss got promoted.

The training department was expanded to include video production, all field employee communications, field IT systems, management training programs, field leadership conferences. I had four managers and dozens of people reporting to me, was flying around the country at the speed of heat and sitting in on high-level client meetings with some pretty major brands. I was on top of a small empire.

Then things started to fall apart at the top. The president of our division was moved into the home corporate offices, my VP was passed over for promotion for the second time and left, several short-term thinkers were promoted and the VP spot was eventually filled by someone who created problems just to be able to solve them. I left to join SPAR Marketing as a VP over human resources and internal operations. A few short years later, Huffy collapsed and the service divisions were sold off in pieces.

SPAR was in Minneapolis so the plan was for me to relocate. A few family emergencies came up during my time at SPAR which caused me to rethink relocating and two years after "moving," I moved back down to Dayton. Since I could not make cars and did not have a security clearance, my employment options were rather limited. I had some graphic design and media skills, so I started up Rivershark Inc. We were a graphic design company for about ten days before we switched to being an Internet company, building out websites and e-strategy solutions.

I have to interrupt my story here to tell you how I came up with the name Rivershark. I actually didn't; my son did. Remember when I told you we spent Saturdays walking down by the Mississippi River? I'm a rambler if you let me and so I was always talking with him. He would point to things in the river and want to know what they were. When I knew, I would tell him—that is a tugboat, a barge, a floating log, a cadaver—but when I didn't, it became a rivershark. Then it was his job to tell me where that rivershark came from, where he was going and what he was going to do on his trip down the river. I would fill in details about the river like the fact that Mark Twain was in St. Louis and he piloted steam boats. He would include these little tidbits in his stories until they become these intricate narratives of one shark's journey down the river.

I was struggling with naming my new media company. "What about Rivershark?" my son says. I added a fin in the "h" and we had a company. He now wants 50% of it and we're still negotiating.

So the lesson here is: If you ever think your kids are not listening to your crazy ramblings, you are wrong. They hear everything.

42

SELLING

I SOLD exercise bikes to paralyzed people
That is the second most interesting thing about me and it is true. Sorta. I received a call from my real estate agent who sold me the house when I relocated to Dayton, as she heard I was back in town. Another client of hers was in the business of some exercise equipment and they were looking for some marketing help. I had worked for Huffy and they did exercise bikes and stuff so perhaps we could do something for each other.

Ok, I bit and set up a meeting to talk with the owner of a company called Electrologic of America. (ELA) He was a good ol' boy from Mississippi who had lived around the world, made a fortune and now found himself owning this bio-medical company that made all sorts of screws and implants that you never, ever want to need. But if you ever found yourself needing them, he was the go-to man.

He paced the room in a very animated strut, while his engineer sat staring at me somewhat bug-eyed, and told me the story about this electronic recumbent bike that allowed paralyzed people to peddle a bike using their own muscles. (True! NASA says so!) Basically, the rider strapped himself in a seat and three sets of electrodes were placed on his hams, quads and gluts. These were hooked into a computer that fired a stimulus, contracting the muscles in the precise order it took to pedal a bike.

I signed up to market and sell them and within three months, we had Christopher Reeve's endorsement as

"The Care for the Cure." I was selling anywhere from seven to nine units a month at $15,000 a piece, half up front, balance due before delivery, no refunds.

To date, that is my best answer ever when asked in a job interview, "So, what makes you qualified for this job?" Ahem. I sold exercise bikes to paralyzed people. You just can't fake that skill.

43

INKSTAINED

After a couple years of selling exercise bikes to paralyzed people, I spun off a line of products aimed at the horse market. Apparently, a condition called "stocking up" was a huge problem, particularly with horses who were being transported by trailer long distances. As I understood it, horse legs are terribly inefficient at circulating blood and the constant contraction and counter-contraction of their leg muscles that kept them upright in a moving trailer contributed to blood and fluid pooling in their legs. That is why trainers walk the horses for several hours after a ride.

I convinced one of the engineers to create a waveform that horses would tolerate and hooked it up to the stim box. Turns out, the horses we tested got addicted to the sensation and couldn't wait to load the trailers and take a ride. Long story short, it worked. We called it Theraquine. (Yeah, I came up with that...)

The longer story is the owners partnered up with a couple of hot-shot marketers out of Maryland, who believed their price and market research more than my gut, and ran the product into the ground. I decided it was time to separate the contract. About that time, a friend of mine got a job in the marketing department at the *Dayton Daily News*.

She called me almost immediately afterward and wanted me to meet with the director of Newspapers In Education. (NIE) They were frustrated with their creative and an inability to execute a grand new plan with the current talent.

By this time, Rivershark was growing quite rapidly and the exercise bike people had been sucking away a lot of my time I should have been spending with other clients and growing out different divisions at Rivershark. I was hesitant to jump into another long-term contract, especially one that required that I be on-site. But, she was persuasive—pestered me constantly—and I relented.

One meeting. Only one and we'll see.

I met with the director of NIE. She explained that while other NIE programs were putting crossword puzzles and mazes on their pages, she wanted to write editorial and educational lesson plans around topics that kids were interested in. She believed that if you respected the kids' intelligence, they would rise to the challenge. She was right; she still is.

Anyone who knows me at least marginally well knows that I love newspapers, old books, typewriters, baked goods and dogs. I've always wanted to work in editorial at a newspaper and this was pretty close. They wanted to hire me as an employee at a salary that made no sense. But I wanted to work there really badly. We compromised on a contract and flexibility and the *Dayton Daily News* NIE program got a bunch of horsepower for chicken feed.

I promised two years; they got four and a half.

During my time at the newspaper, I had the opportunity to work with the most creative, dedicated and smart group of individuals I have ever known. We changed the world slightly, even though it was only for a few short years.

Aside from the great NIE team at the newspaper, working at the newspaper also gave me a great 9/11 story. The website person had gone home for the day (this is when newspapers only updated their web sites once a day and everything was done at night, after the print edition was put to bed.) Apparently, I was the only one in the building who could create, post and manage website content independently.

The photo editor at that time, Jeff Adams †, raced

down to my floor and asked my director to "borrow" me for the day, or until they could reach the website producer and get her back in to work. From about 9:30am until 4:00pm, I was updating www.DaytonDailyNews.com, pulling off photos and 9/11 stories from the AP wire and posting updates as fast as we could. In 2001, the CNN.com servers were overwhelmed and people were turning to their local newspaper websites for updates. That event—while tragic—single-handedly changed local newspaper internet strategy.

I remember the day going slow and fast all at the same time. I remember how calm and professional the newsroom was, how the entire team become hyper-focused on getting local news coverage, processing photos and assembling the "bulldog" edition of the newspaper. I remember seeing a deluge of news stories on the AP wire still happening everywhere else in the world that nobody anywhere was reporting.

I remember stepping out into downtown Dayton from the Ludlow *Dayton Daily News* bank building and how quiet traffic was and how slowly everyone walked.

I went home. And went to work the next day. And the next and the next. Everything changed, but nothing changed.

44

SOCCER KICKS IN

I HAD BEFRIENDED AN OLDER MARKETING artist, Jim, whose career had changed rapidly from bluelines and Xacto knives to Macs, QuarkXPress and digital proofs. I could tell he was struggling with the technology after having had an almost thirty-year career in old style advertising layout. He was an extraordinarily kind person and—unlike many older newsies—he was open to learning new skills, even as he did not quite understand them. I had a lot of software training skills and helped him where I could with the technical stuff, building his confidence in his skills. With a 30+ year career at the advertising department at the *Dayton Daily News*, he knew people within the community and those people trusted him.

"What does Rivershark do," Jim asked me once. I told him mostly what we are doing right now is building these exciting jobbank tools to help find merchandisers for this new trade association called NARMS (Now the World Alliance for Retail Excellence & Standards) This was before Google, before Craig's List, before LinkedIn or anyone else really doing a job bank that had a high level of specificity. The *only* jobs that were there were real jobs from NARMS members.

We also built a database for retail merchandisers where NARMS member could search by geography and skills. Within a year, we had over 100,000 merchandisers in the database and over half the NARMS members were signed up to search it. It was the de facto place on the internet for find a retail merchandising jobs.

"Could you do the same for soccer tournaments?" he asked. "I guess we could do something like that."

Later that week he had a meeting with the Warrior Soccer Club to talk about the DDN ad placement for their annual adidas Warrior Soccer Tournament. Unbeknownst to me, he pitched me as a guy who could help them build a cool website for their tournament.

It didn't go anywhere. They weren't ready.

The summer came and went and I ended it beginning my daughter's soccer season with a now defunct pre-season tournament, the Northmont Bolt Cup. We were given paper maps and schedules the day before by our coach. When I got to the soccer tournament with my daughter, I had no idea where she had to play or what time she needed to be there. The maps were all wrong and there was no place to check the schedule. Through dumb luck, I found her team and she didn't miss her game.

There had to be a better way.

I went home after the two games she played, looked at the software that was running the NARMS website and figured I had written enough code to create a system that could register teams, manage the applications and do some marketing. The scheduling and scoring parts would have to be done, but I was confident it could be. It had to be done.

That Monday morning, I was re-telling my soccer tournament frustrations with Jim over lunch and he reminded me of our conversation several months ago. "If I could put together a pitch deck," he said, "he could get a meeting with the Warrior folks."

About a week later, we found ourselves in the lobby of a Max&Erma's with me, Jim and my laptop, staring at about ten folks from the Warrior Soccer Club. We all squeezed around a table; Jim introduced me to Carol and Jim P, the co-directors of the Warrior Classic, and I was off, pitching the new www.warriorclassic.com.

I got about 4–5 slides into it and Carol asked, "How much?"

"It was free to the tournament," I said, "we'll recoup

from the traffic and ads," which was the internet business model of the day.

"Do it," Carol said.

And like an idiot who forgot to shut up when I got to a 'yes,' I said, "But I got more slides to show you!"

And with that, TourneyCentral was born.

45

THE RULES OF A JOB

IN THE WORDS of Bertram Cooper[1], there are other rules. These are the other rules.

Every so often, the yoots[2] will get career advice from the olds. Most of it is rubbish so the kids assume all of it is rubbish ... quit rolling your eyes at me, Kyle! This will be the one and only time I'm gonna publish my rubbish. Also, technology changes; people don't. Study people and acquire tech skills as you need them. In that order.

The immutable rules of a job are thus:

Your job exists either to make the company money or save the company money. Sometimes there is some crossover of the two, but rarely until you get up into the management/leadership ranks.

Everybody at the company has a boss. The lower down the chain you are, the more bosses your boss has. The further up the chain you go, the more bosses you have.

This one is a tough one, but the more you understand it, the more successful you will be. NOBODY should give a sh*t more about the tasks you need to do or the outcomes of your job more than you, whether you grill burgers, assemble bicycles, solve IT problems, perform

---

1. Please don't ask me who Bertram Cooper is. Google, ChatCPT, TikTok it or whatever it is your generation does to find out stuff these days. But don't be satisfied with your ignorance. Have you read nothing the past two minutes?
2. Google "My Cousin Vinny" for this generational and demographic reference.

live music for millions, plan conferences, raise money for dog shelters, clean up vomit or plan strategy for global logistics. This isn't to say you should accept being overworked and exploited—giving a sh*t and accepting abuse is not the same thing, helps to know the difference—but nobody should give a sh*t[3] more than you about those things of your job.

Your boss cares, but if they have to care MORE than you, you are giving them stress they don't need or want. After all, they have their own boss who expects they should give a sh*t about the tasks and outcomes of their job more than their boss.

You can argue, but you'd be wrong. Until you understand it and make peace with it, you'll be a source of friction for your boss, the company and yourself.

Change is annoying. Your suggestions for change will be met with resistance, even when you have a C-job. But work on it anyway, just don't tell anyone. Don't ask permission to start thinking about what changes could be made, how they would be implemented or paid for ... BUT don't suggest them until your plan is fully formed and you've figured out to produce some outcomes with a few trial runs nobody noticed you do. Preparation meets opportunity is almost always the best road to change things in a lasting, meaningful way.

You'll throw away more plans than you'll execute. But make them anyway.

Lastly, don't expect credit for anything. Accept it when given, but don't expect it. Don't get bitter when your boss takes credit for stuff you do because YOU are one of the outcomes of their job. Again, don't accept abuse, but also accept your performance is one of your boss's outcomes.

There are a lot of other nuanced immutable rules[2] of a job—like how like-ability will always win out over skill—but these are foundational.

---

3. "Give a sh*t" defined as figuring out how things work, getting what you need from people and systems, getting skilled, efficient and effective, just handle it, not waiting to be told what to do, learn ... learn more, figuring out and executing being pleasant to work with... there's probably more but this is enough. "Sweep your side of the street."

46

INANIMATE ME

"If a pastry plate sitting on the table of a weekend cable news show could talk, what would it say?"

MOST THINGS worth doing start with a question. That was the question I asked myself before launching into what could arguably be the most silly, yet oddly rewarding, venture of my media career. With this question rattling around in my head, I found my next adventure.

Off to the twitters!

In September of 2011, MSNBC launched an untested format in cable news—the television version of the long-form essay—aptly named *UP with Chris Hayes* because it aired from 8-10am ET. A small but loyal group of viewers and fans started watching and quickly adopted the hashtag #uppers. I counted myself among these early adopters.

All winter, every weekend, I watched with the #uppers hashtag trending every weekend. I established the @UpPastryPlate account on twitter, tweeted out I was baking for next weekend and I was a real, live sentient object. We established the hashtag #pastriot and awarded it to guests who were caught by the live, on-air cameras eating from the pastry plate. It became a very big deal within the #uppers community, even becoming a game of cat-and-mouse between the guests and the control room.

That next month, *LA Food Weekly* came out with an article on Chris Hayes, which mentions the Pastry Plate, they go out and find my twitter handle, publish it and I saw a little over a thousand new followers within the day.

Chris Hayes eventually moved into prime time in 2013 with his show *All In with Chris Hayes*, in part fueled by the popularity created by a few hundred thousand fans called #uppers who hooked into a conversation and community they found in the Pastry Plate. Steve Kornacki took over the *UP* host seat and adopted the Plate as a "mascot," cementing the brand even further.

The account even led to a presentation at SXSW in March of 2015, discussing whether anonymity can be authentic. It can and almost always is.

Eventually, MSNBC cancelled the show at the end of 2015 as talent contracts expired and Andy Lack tried moving the weekend format more toward rolling coverage.

At that point, I moved the @UpPastryPlate into the more generic @PastryPlate account and continued tweeting as a free agent, retaining a large contingent of #uppers and slowly gaining new members.

In October of 2017, while walking my dogs in the park, I received a text from one of the MSNBC producers who knew I was from the Chris and Steve days, asking if I would be interested in supporting a new *UP* show with the @UpPastryPlate account.

"Heck yeah! When do we start?"

The new *UP* used the same format, with David Gura—formerly of NPR—as the host. We ran for another 18 months, with the eventual cancel—again—in January of 2019. David's sign-off acknowledged the contributions of the Pastry Plate which was a big hit with the fans and friends of the show.

In every case, Chris, Steve and David knew my real identity, even as they were sworn to secrecy[1] from their co-workers and producers. It was a bit of fun, a bit of mystery that went with creating the illusion of a sentient pastry plate. Of course, everybody knew there was a human being behind the account, but staying in character was critical for the illusion to work.

---

1. And now you know. Use this knowledge wisely.

The Plate was much more than a silly foray into the insane world of cable television politics. To have developed the character of a sentient pastry plate over seven+ years, spanning over 240,000 tweets and guiding a community along online as the show broadcast live and not learned anything, would be a waste of time.

- People have a craving to belong to a community, to be heard and seen. The Plate tried hard to be true to that need, replying, liking or RTing as fast as possible during the live show as well as responding between segments on commercial breaks.
- Guests need validation, especially elected officials. More than once, a producer would DM me, saying that the guest asked, "What did the Pastry Plate tweet about me?" Every guest checked their twitter feed either during breaks or immediately after their hit.
- The Plate was personal to many people at home. One #upper in particular would watch *UP* with her mom during visits at hospice, saying her mom and her enjoyed laughing at the tweets and following along, that she died happy. It continues to awe and humble me, knowing that there was a real person behind every tweet. It shaped the conversation within a human context, not just bits on the screen going into a void.
- Playing the character of an inanimate object on twitter is hard. The first week, you run out of pastry puns and you better have something else to sustain that character. It takes improv and repartee skills in abundance. Knowing lots of trivia also helps; not Ken Jennings stuff, but pretty darn close. Fortunately, I had more than ten years prior, playing a dog on the internet @dogwalkblog

Now that *Up on MSNBC* has been retired, (for now) I continue to play the part of the Pastry Plate, interested in the intersection of pastry, politics and pop culture.

47

HITTING THE GROUND RUNNING

Recently, someone posted up a question in Quora, asking what one does with an English Lit degree. It reminded me of an essay I wrote a while back, parts of which I will share with you here.

AT THAT TIME, there was a narrative going on within the creative community lamenting the demise of professional graphic artists.

Inevitably, someone brings up *Mad Men* as an example of the glory days of advertising.

And I sigh deeply.

Firstly, let's get one thing perfectly clear; Don Draper is a fictional character, partially based on Draper Daniels, the creative head of the Chicago-based Leo Burnett advertising agency in the '50s. Matt Weiner can write him to do anything and say anything. He did not exist. He does not exist. Never. Ever, ever, ever.

Don's story for us starts *in medias res* as a successful creative director banging out copy in a bar in New York City. As the story unfolds over the next four seasons, we find out he was a poor kid growing up on a farm "somewhere in the Midwest," joined the Army to get the heck off the farm, sold used cars in California, never went to college, never wrote anything longer than 250 words, moved to New York City, sold furs and did copywriting/advertising on the side for the owner (who probably never would have hired a graphic artist if Don didn't do the work) and eventually grifted his way into Sterling-Cooper.

Don's path is hardly the one you most read about. Most professional graphic artists have a BFA or certificate from an art school. They trained to eventually become creative/art directors in agencies, living the Don Draper Dream. This is how all the job descriptions read, probably even yours.

But if you look closely, the credentialed people who work at Sterling-Cooper and later Sterling-Cooper-Draper-Price are the first ones getting fired when an account is lost. Don prevails and gets stronger despite not having the credentials of a "real" creative director. Sure, he has his moments of panic but who doesn't? And Don's panic is more understandable when he admits to himself he has been faking his entire adult life. Again, folks, he is not real so Weiner can write all these traits into the Don Draper character.

The problem with not believing Don Draper isn't real is I *know* people like Don Draper. You probably do, too. I know people in the graphic arts field who have no business being there because they don't have the "proper" credentials. Yet, they are the folks I turn to when I need something done.

How many agencies would hire a Don Draper if he was looking for work? Probably all of them. How many would hire a used-car salesman turned furrier who did advertising for them on the side without an art degree? None of them. The irony in all this is the latter is exactly what Sterling-Cooper did, albeit unknowingly.

Don was successful not so much because of his superior copywriting and creative ability, but in his willingness to learn and his keen observation of human behavior. He learned what made people tick and more importantly, how to make them tick to a rhythm he tapped out. He played Roger into his job and continued to play him through the last episode. For Don, Roger is the perfect whetstone that sharpens his skills. But this is not a character analysis essay; this is just a reminder that creative ability is not about art degrees. Creative people don't hold any special rights to the keys of knowledge;

but people who are willing to use the tools they have and sharpen that craft, do.

Like the graphic arts industry, *Mad Men* could have easily just evaporated after season four. The most ardent fans among us would have had a momentary Don Draper panic moment, but then like Don, realized life goes in only one direction—forward. Instead of slinking home in the rain to a stiff drink and a pair of bedroom slippers, we would have sighed deeply, been grateful for the spectacular opportunity we had been given, looked bravely onto the horizon and enthusiastically asked:

"What's next?"

Everyone in advertising wants to *be* Don Draper but few want to go through the pain of *becoming* Don. Fewer still want the anxiety of *staying* Don.

MY PERSONAL DON JOURNEY

Every job listing wants the prospective employee to "hit the ground running." I don't really know what that means exactly, other than they want to hire you, plunk you down at a work station or in front of a team and have you start producing results. Ok, I get it. That's the career game, isn't it?

But the irony in all this is every company is different, every job is slightly different; even the same job I may have done with a competitor. But *you* hired **me**, so you want more than what I did for them over there because your company is better. That's why we're here and that's why you are reading my story.

You want me for my grifting skills. You want me for my ability to learn now to adapt what I know and make us both better than our past.

I'll be the first to admit I grifted my way into many jobs. I had to, we all had to; companies were looking for experience and I couldn't get experience unless I got a job… it's pretty much the age-old Catch-22 anyone faces who is looking to start out or remake a career.

I don't know how other people have done it, but here some highlights of my personal "career grift." I am sharing these secrets with you; treat them wisely.

1. I didn't know how to cook at 15 when I got my first weekend chef job. But I learned because I had been asking the day chef to let me help prep food after my shifts as a dishwasher. He eventually gave me an apron, a set of knifes and upgraded my paper hat to a cloth chef hat.
2. I didn't know how to manage a stocking crew at a major retailer, but I apparently gave off vibes of knowing how to organize a crew and manage the logistics of a dock and storeroom. Early mornings, fast-paced work and shoving pallets of product into impossibly tight spaces in the storeroom, but I was boss of all of it.
3. I didn't know how to assemble and repair bicycles but I learned and practiced taking bikes apart and putting them back together until I was as fast and accurate as Forrest Gump tearing down a sidearm.
4. I didn't know how to staff up a crew of techs when they gave me a metro to manage or how to achieve profitability but I learned that when you get employees to trust you by doing what you promise, they will perform in the field with minimal to no supervision. I exceeded sales plans and lowered warranty repairs so much they shipped me into the Dayton Office to replicate my methods company-wide.
5. I had no idea how to create a comprehensive training program or build a digital video department (c. 1992) but I learned. We made our own training videos in house at 1/10 the cost of outside vendors.
6. I had no idea how to sell exercise bikes to paralyzed people. But I figured it out by listening and learning the language, the process and what formerly active people who suddenly find themselves paralyzed think and feel. Today, I'm a foremost expert on FES. Ask me anything.

7. I didn't even know how to use QuarkXpress when I told a newspaper I did. I had used Pagemaker, how different could it be? The keystrokes and nomenclature were slightly different, but the design concepts were the same.
8. I did not know how to create database-driven websites to create the leading soccer tournament SaaS in the US, but I figured it out and tapped into some smart people who showed me the ropes.

But I did go to college and get an English degree. That is one thing I didn't have to lie about... well, except for the part about never being about to do anything with a worthless English degree. That is and always will be, a lie.

48

WHAT IS THE WHEELBASE OF A CAT?

Sarah Wilson-Blackwell wrote a book about SEO titled, "Heavy Traffic, Drive Organic Traffic to your Website with SEO Content Writing," and it is as funny as it is informative. If I did not include this "viral, number one at Google" story in a legacy book, what have I really been doing with my life? Anyway, here it is...

Sarah Wilson-Blackwell's book, Heavy Traffic, Drive Organic Traffic to your Website with SEO Content Writing, is as funny as it is informative. She delivers what promises to be a dry, boring, mundane, pedantic subject in a delightfully light, deadpan cadence.

Her irreverent, snarky tone is a delight with every turn of the page, leading the reader further down the rabbit hole of her brain.

If her goal was to merely sell a book, she would have already succeeded. Once the reader has turned the first page, however, she has further succeeded in dragging them into a world she views a little off-kilter from the obvious and into the subtle shadows the light creates. There is no option for the reader to escape other than to power through to the end.

The reward is a curiosity, not simply about SEO, but about the connection of disparate things. You will emerge with odd questions you need to know the answer to, like the wheelbase of a cat.

I googled "what is the wheelbase of a cat" and oddly, I got no results. There are other things people measure on their cat, like neck size, chest girth, etc, but in the entirety of the existence of the human race, it appears nobody has ever measured the wheelbase of a cat.

And the SEO keyword "wheelbase of a cat" has not been indexed in Google.

Until now.

Buy her book. Keep the curiosity about your world alive.

Sarah's book.

49

THE SMELL OF SUN AND WARM BODIES

I FIRST THOUGHT that these essays inside the box would be all anger and not any shred of happiness and so far I have not been proven wrong. But one thing I keep focusing on in my life is not about pain or anger or injustice or loss of purpose or autonomy, though there is plenty of all that to go around—but the absence of JOY! Where did Joy go?

Where did my ability to see and feel good stuff go? Where did it go for all of us? Why is everything now a chore instead of something we have the luck and privilege to do?

I have to do the laundry. I have to write that letter. I have to bang out that essay. I have to create that recording.

I have to produce that podcast. I have to go to work. I have to go to your birthday party. I have to edit that manuscript. I have to... insert any number of things here and everything is a chore. Where did the joy of feeling the outside sun on your face go? Or the feeling of dirt on your hands? The joy of feeling warm water rush across your skin, the smell of clean soap in your hair? The rush of wind across your chest. The feel of your throat tighten as each word escapes onto the page, your eyeballs furtively watching the horror of your thoughts spill onto the page, helpless to stop the carnage. Don't say THAT, your brain screams to nobody listening. Yet, here it is... naked thoughts with nobody stepping up to defend them. Where is JOY??? Did I not feed you well? Did I not give you enough ammunition to fight these other feelings?

Was I that short-sighted? Have I left you on the battlefield, alone, naked and afraid?

To weekends where cell phones did not exist, where sand and sun and warm bodies and the smell of sunscreen did, where the roads felt smooth and curvy and the wind in my hair and my eyes.

I think about entire Sundays were spent on the beach, sand everywhere during and days afterwards... the smell of skin warmed by the sun, massaged by coconut sunscreen.

No notifications, no phones ringing, no anxiety of the server being down... no blockade to joy, when I owned my time and space, my own thoughts which were always where I was. Always...

YOU ARE HERE. And here we are now, apologizing for feeling any joy, guilty for not spending those extra few minutes grinding out on some pointless software that is exceedingly awesome and under-appreciated for what it is, always missing that one feature that was expected but never expressed. You must suck because I think your thing here sucks... I alone get to determine how much you are worth based on my unexpressed expectations ...

Did you not get my text? Why were you not glued to your phone so that I can pump misery straight into your eyeballs and earholes?

Why were you cheating on me with Joy? You are supposed to be miserable all the time. You long too much for a past that is gone.

But is it?

Does it really need to be? How did all THIS become normal? What if I chose it not to be? How does one even do that today? The phone does not come with an off switch and I have now leaked beyond the box and not found Joy...

> I first thought that these essays inside the box would be all anger unless
> and not any sored of happiness and so far I have not been proven wrong.
> /xx/ But one thing I keep focusing on in my life is not about pain or anger
> injustice or less of purpose or autonomy. xxxxx through there is plenty
> of all that to go around ... but the absence of JOY!! Where did joy go?
> Where did my ability to see and feel good stuff go? Where did it go for
> all of us? Why is everything now a chore instead of something we have the
> luck and privlege to do? I /xx/ have to do the laundry. I have to write that
> letter, I have to bang out that essay. I have to create that recording,
> I have to produce that podcast, I have to go to work. I have to go to xx/
> your birthday party. I have to edit that manuscript. I have to... In ert
> any number of things here and everything is a chore. Where did the joy of
> feeling the outside sun on your bare go? Or the feeling of dirt on xx/
> your hands? The joy of feeling warm water rush across your skin, the smell
> of clean soap in your hair? The rush of wind across your chest. The feel
> of typewriter keys spring and release from your fingertip, the smell of
> the x/ ink, the age of the dust as your breathing quick as and xx////
> your throat tightens a few hard escapes onto the page, your eyeballs
> festive in watching the mirror of your thoughts spill onto the page.//x/xx
> helpless to stop the carnage. Don't say xx THAT, your brain screams to
> nobody listening. Yet, here it is... naked thoughts with nobody stepping
> up to defend them. Where is JOY??? Did I not feed you well? Did I not
> give you enough ambitions to fight? Were other feelings? Was I that
> short-sighted? Have I left you on the battlefield, alone, naked and afraid?
> I think about you often, Joy, where you went and how to get you back. When
> I think Joy, I think xx back to weekends where cell phones did not exist
> where sand and sun and warm bodies and the smell of suns reen did. Where
> the roads felt a sooth and curvy and the wind in my hair and my eyes ...
> I think xxxx about entire Sundays xxxxx spent on the beach, sand everywhere
> during and days afterwards... the smell of skin warmed by the sun, massaged
> by xxxxx coconut sunscreen. To notifications, no phones ringing, no
> anxiety of the server being down... no blocade to joy. Simple, I owned
> my time and space, my own thoughts which were always where I was. Always...
> xxx YOU ARE HERE. And here we are now, apologizing for feeling any joy,
> guilty for not spending those extra few minutes grinding out on software
> software that is excessively awesome and underappreciated for what it is,
> alwaysmissing that one feature that was expected but never expressed. Xu/
> You must suck because I think you r /xxx thing here sucks... I alone get
> to determine how much you are worth based on my unexpressed expectations ...
> Did you not get my text? Why were you not glued to your phone so that I
> can pump misery xxxxxxxxxx straight into your eyeballs and earholes?
> Why were you ghosting on me with JOY? You are supposed to be miserable
> all the time. You long too much for a past that is gone. But is it?
> Does it really need to be? How did all THIS become normal? What if I chose
> it not to be? How does one even do that today? The phone does not come
> with an off switch and I have not looked beyond the box and not found joy...

Essay part of the typewriter in a square project by the author.

50

THE REAL SH*T

When other people ask me what I do, what my story is, they get the previous chapters. The following chapter is the story that people don't want to hear when they say they want to know who I am.

I WAS BORN in Minnesota as the second of five in a working class family. I grew up in the shadows of a slum neighborhood in St. Paul known as Frogtown. At the end of our street were four bars, one a biker bar. My family was so poor that we "shopped" at the Goodwill for second-hand clothing. I distinctly remember one very cold winter where I had only a green sort of plaid cloth coat to keep me warm. My cheeks, ears and fingers were frost-bitten one morning while walking to school, scars I bear still today.

When I was nine years old, I lied to the *St. Paul Pioneer Press and Dispatch* saying I was ten—their minimum age—to get three paper routes. I delivered papers every morning and evening. The money went towards food and school tuition. (*I attended St. Agnes Catholic School. My parents wanted to give us kids a good education, but they could not afford it. This was my only option to stay in a good school.*)

The daily walk to school and back was also quite dangerous, having to pass by several neighborhoods that were less than affluent. There were bullies on almost every block who took pride is chasing and beating up on kids who wore Catholic school uniforms. There were no busses for us to ride and asking our parents to walk with us was not really an option with babies at home. We toughened up quickly; some fights we lost, some fights we won. But every day, there was a struggle of some kind.

I START WORKING A REAL JOB

When I turned 14, I got a job at the Viking Village Smorgasbord as a busboy for $2.30/hour. My mom took over the paper routes to keep the income flowing into our family. My dad was a claims clerk for Ingersoll, but lost his job in a merger. He went on to create three businesses, which ultimately failed, not for lack of trying, however. They eventually divorced.

By the time I was 15, almost 16, I made my way from a busboy to the head weekend cook, arriving in the pre-dawn hours and leaving when the sun set every Saturday and Sunday. I also worked almost every weekday. I was thrilled when I got a raise to $3.10/hour!

All the while I was working, I was keeping up a 4.0 GPA at school, taking advanced math, science and language classes. If you research St. Agnes High School, you will discover that was no small accomplishment. I graduated eighth in my class. There were a lot of smart kids in my graduating class and the competition was fierce. We were all friends, fighting the same battles for good grades that got us into good colleges, so it was all good.

My transportation to and from work was a bus that ran on University Ave, from Dale St. to Snelling Ave. At that time, the drop off and pick up corner was an infamous hooker and peep-show corner, with nude dancing theaters. Almost every night when I got off work —smelling of fry grease and garbage—I was propositioned. I was 14-16 years old, but it didn't matter to them. The hookers were also desperate for money and I was a potential john.

Sometimes I walked to work, but the neighborhoods I needed to cross through were more dangerous and unpalatable than the bus. Yet, every day I went to work to pay for basic life needs and school tuition.

At 17, I was lucky enough to get a job at the new Target Store (T160.) It was in the same neighborhood, but the place was changing. The St. Paul Police cleaned out one of the strip joints (The Belmont Club) and made it into a police station.

By then, I had purchased a car and was driving, but not before I threatened my dad with physical violence for him to sign my driving license application. I'm not proud of that, but it was necessary. It haunts me to this day I chose that path; I saw no other option.

LAUNCHING INTO LIFE

When I graduated high school, I started my studies at the University of Minnesota, even testing out of several math, science and language requirements. I studied Latin taught by nuns for four years in high school. I worked 40 hour plus every week at Target for two years in college, got married and had a son. I dropped out of the traditional college track and began going to night school, carrying 12-16 credit hours when I was offered a full time management job with Target, mostly because it came with great health insurance.

After 6 ½ years of working at Target, I was then offered a job with YLCE (Later, Huffy Service first) assembling bicycles for retail stores. I took it because it paid better and the hours were more flexible. It was hard work, but I got most weekends off and I could expand my college classes in the morning, work through the day and go to a night class. In the winter, when bikes were less in demand (Minnesota winters!) I studied harder to finish my degree.

MOVING ACROSS THE COUNTRY

After building bikes for almost three years, Huffy offered me an area management job, which later turned into a promotion and relocation to Dayton, Ohio. I thought I had finished my degree, but found out after moving, I was four credit hours short. I was furious, but it was what it was.

I later finished remotely by fast-talking a professor at Wright State University to be an advisor and my English undergrad advisor at the University of Minnesota was flexible. For those two kind souls, I will be forever grateful. They didn't have to go out of their way to help someone they barely knew, on a problem that wasn't theirs to solve, but they did.

Three months prior to relocating, my daughter was born. It was a hectic time as our house was trying to sell when the first Gulf War broke out. Nobody was buying houses because nobody was certain of the economy. It eventually sold, but not after 121 showings and several Minnesota March blizzards that forced a very pregnant woman to clear the long and wide driveway with a snow blower. I was living temporarily in Dayton as my job started in January and we finally sold the house in June. The folks at Huffy were unbelievably understanding of my situation and for them, I am also grateful.

The job at Huffy required a lot of travel, which means I missed a lot of time with my daughter, but that is what a corporate job entails. We give up some things to be able to provide for our families, health insurance being one of those things. After working at Huffy for several years and securing several promotions, I was offered a VP position with a marketing company back in Minneapolis.

Before we could relocate, my mother in-law—who lived in Denmark—passed away. I commuted back and forth between Dayton and Minneapolis for as long as I could, but it soon became apparent that relocation was out of the question. I did what every responsible dad and husband would do; I moved back to Dayton where I was resolved to make it my home until my two kids were out of college.

I SELL EXERCISE BIKES TO PARALYZED PEOPLE

After moving back to Dayton, I took a job with a local medical device firm and sold exercise bikes to paralyzed people for over two years before "grifting" my way into a position with the *Dayton Daily News*. On 9/11, I was at the website desk, updating the site as news flowed in from CNN and the AP. I was tasked with this because I was the only one in the building at that time who had website skills. It was both awesome and humbling to be the public voice of calm through a chaotic day.

All the while I was working at the bio-medical company and the newspaper, I was building a business on nights, weekends and the wee hours of the morning. I have an entrepreneurial spirit that needed to soar.

ON MY OWN

In 2002, I was able to work full-time on my business. I am a job creator, having created fourteen verifiable jobs since 2002, including my own. I built a company that is the second largest soccer tournament management firm in the country. I am very proud of this accomplishment.

The first consideration to working my company full-time was being able to provide health insurance for my family. I was lucky to happen upon an insurance broker who walked me through a plan that covered my family and was affordable. It is the plan I have still today, but only because of the protections the ACA afforded me after 2010-2014. It is quite expensive now, and the benefits have dropped slightly, but at least I have health insurance.

Income from my company also allowed me to send my two kids to college and gave me the flexibility to be there to support them when writing a 20-page paper was almost unbearable. It was a tough time, taking on demanding clients, but it was money; money I needed to provide education, a safe home, food, clothing and health insurance. They both graduated from Ohio Universities, Miami University with a BFA and Wright State University with a BA in History. They have both since moved out of Ohio—New York and Houston, respectively. It makes me sad every day they are not close to me, but there are no jobs in Ohio that will allow them to live their potential. They are very bright and Dayton would just hold them back.

My daughter is student debt-free and my son has minimal student loans which I am helping him pay off, as I was committed to help them through college. Wright State is less expensive than Miami, but I understand artists. He is a very talented artist and his soul needed that nourishment. A college degree is a minimum requirement for today's work force. It also expands intellectual curiosity and earnings potential. It allows my kids to see a world beyond their immediate surroundings. You understand.

WRITING

In the time since I started working full-time on my company, I wrote four books, one of which is *100 letters to Hillary Clinton* on my health care. along with the first legacy volume, *Monkey with a Loaded Typewriter*. I am working on a fifth, the second legacy volume. If you are reading this, I have also accomplished that goal.

In 2013, I was hit hard unexpectedly with a bout of CIDP, which affected the nerves throughout my body. I was lucky in some ways because I built a flexible business that afforded me income. I had the good fortune to have a doctor who cared enough to poke around for care. I was patched up by some exceptional doctors at Ohio State University, doctors I will be grateful to for the rest of my life. I'm not 100% and probably never will be, but I am able to make a living with my head instead of my back.

I am sharing this story because I am one such "rags to riches American Dream" story Americans believe. I believe in hard work, personal responsibility, education and dignity through purpose.

But something changed with American culture. It became selfish. It became a culture of taking away rights to those who worked hard to build companies, provide for families and squirrel away a bit for retirement to be able to enjoy the company of grandkids in relative comfort one day.

Here is the rub. I am a middle-aged, white man living in the Rust Belt of America; a small-businessman who created a company from nothing but hard work, education, sweat, help from others, entrepreneurial efforts and an indomitable spirit that created jobs and lots of tax revenue to the various tax agencies. I am a homeowner in the suburbs of Dayton. I raised two kids and educated them through college. **I am very proud of these accomplishments even as our insatiable culture demands more.**

MY FUTURE

The last decades of my life will not be anything like I had planned nor will the lives of my two kids. I don't know the details of my life plan, but I am the same unsinkable ship as when I was nine years old and I will endure. I will adjust my sails.

We are all on this planet together; ***what affects you affects me.*** That is my life mantra, my North Star.

ABOUT GERARD

Gerard Mclean is a humor essayist disguised as a writer. He has written several essay collections, some technical manuals, way more tweets than is healthy and more than his fair share of letters. While much of his work is considered by many to be humorous, in this work, he is just being real.

A small business owner and author of four books, Gerard moved from the American states of Minnesota to Ohio in 1991. The father of two adult kids, both of whom were raised and educated in Ohio, is an avid chronicler of life who is intent on leaving a legacy to the world in the stories he identifies as being meaningful in some way.

No intentional comedy is contained within.

@gerardmclean at most of these places.
gerardmclean.com always. Visit at your own peril.

ALSO BY GERARD MCLEAN

Monkey with a Loaded Typewriter
The Game Through Glass
Dear Hillary; 100 Letters about health care
A Face for Radio and a Voice for Twitter

www.ingramcontent.com/pod-product-compliance
Lightning Source LLC
Chambersburg PA
CBHW060611080526
44585CB00013B/773